VENICE SIMPLON ORIENT-EXPRESS

The continental rake of the Venice Simplon-Orient-Express.

Shirley Sherwood

VENICE SIMPLON ORIENT-EXPRESS

THE RETURN OF THE WORLD'S MOST CELEBRATED TRAIN

WEIDENFELD & NICOLSON
London

The British Pullmans on the way to Folkestone.

Designed by Trevor Vincent for
George Weidenfeld & Nicolson Limited 91 Clapham High Street London sw4

Maps drawn by Brian and Constance Dear

Picture editor   Julia Brown

ISBN 0 297 78261 4

Colour separations by Newsele Ltd

Phototypeset by Keyspools Ltd, Golborne, Lancs
Printed and bound in Italy by L.E.G.O. Vicenza

CONTENTS

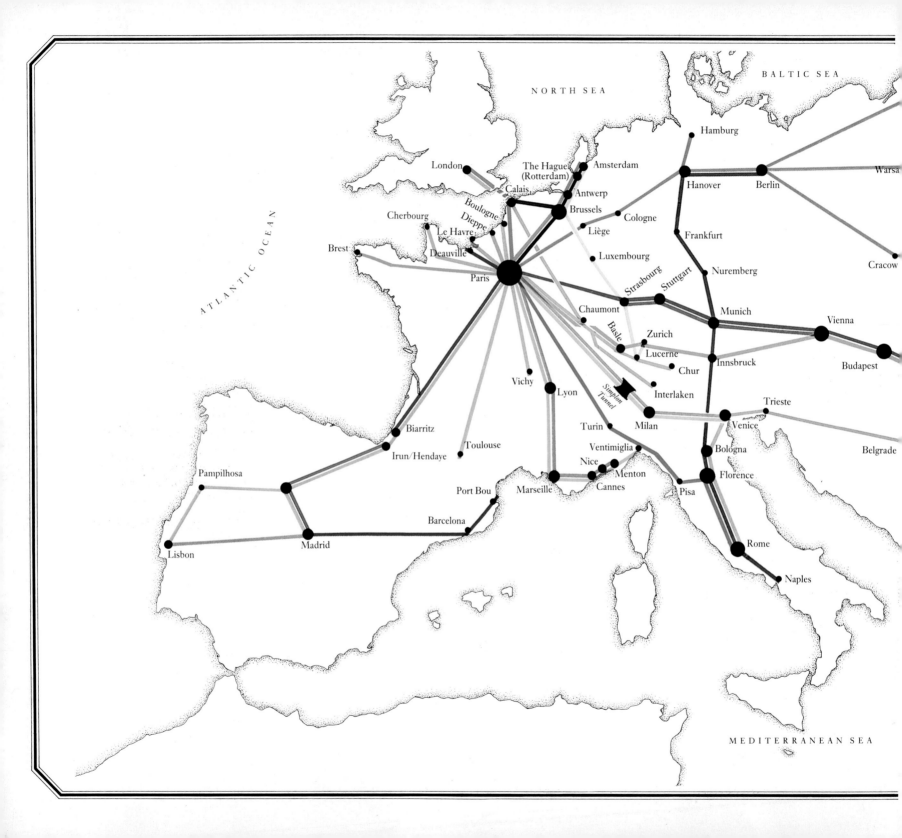

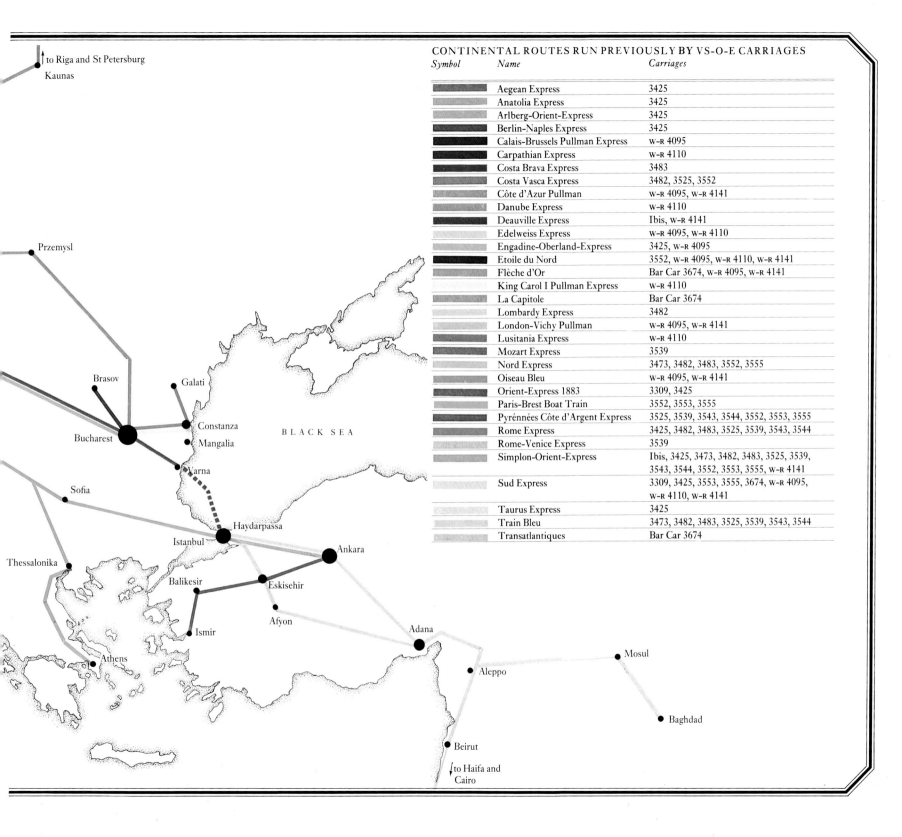

to Riga and St Petersburg

Kaunas

Przemysl

Brasov

Galati

Bucharest

Constanza

Mangalia

BLACK SEA

Varna

Sofia

Haydarpassa

Istanbul

Ankara

Thessalonika

Balikesir

Eskisehir

Afyon

Ismir

Adana

Mosul

Aleppo

Athens

Baghdad

Beirut

to Haifa and
Cairo

CONTINENTAL ROUTES RUN PREVIOUSLY BY VS-O-E CARRIAGES

Symbol	Name	Carriages
	Aegean Express	3425
	Anatolia Express	3425
	Arlberg-Orient-Express	3425
	Berlin-Naples Express	3425
	Calais-Brussels Pullman Express	w-r 4095
	Carpathian Express	w-r 4110
	Costa Brava Express	3483
	Costa Vasca Express	3482, 3525, 3552
	Côte d'Azur Pullman	w-r 4095, w-r 4141
	Danube Express	w-r 4110
	Deauville Express	Ibis, w-r 4141
	Edelweiss Express	w-r 4095, w-r 4110
	Engadine-Oberland-Express	3425, w-r 4095
	Etoile du Nord	3552, w-r 4095, w-r 4110, w-r 4141
	Flèche d'Or	Bar Car 3674, w-r 4095, w-r 4141
	King Carol I Pullman Express	w-r 4110
	La Capitole	Bar Car 3674
	Lombardy Express	3482
	London-Vichy Pullman	w-r 4095, w-r 4141
	Lusitania Express	w-r 4110
	Mozart Express	3539
	Nord Express	3473, 3482, 3483, 3552, 3555
	Oiseau Bleu	w-r 4095, w-r 4141
	Orient-Express 1883	3309, 3425
	Paris-Brest Boat Train	3552, 3553, 3555
	Pyrénnées Côte d'Argent Express	3525, 3539, 3543, 3544, 3552, 3553, 3555
	Rome Express	3425, 3482, 3483, 3525, 3539, 3543, 3544
	Rome-Venice Express	3539
	Simplon-Orient-Express	Ibis, 3425, 3473, 3482, 3483, 3525, 3539, 3543, 3544, 3552, 3553, 3555, w-r 4141
	Sud Express	3309, 3425, 3553, 3555, 3674, w-r 4095, w-r 4110, w-r 4141
	Taurus Express	3425
	Train Bleu	3473, 3482, 3483, 3525, 3539, 3543, 3544
	Transatlantiques	Bar Car 3674

BRITISH ROUTES RUN PREVIOUSLY BY VS-O-E PULLMANS

Symbol	Name	Carriages
	Bournemouth Belle	Ione, Zena
	Brighton Belle	Audrey
	Devon Belle	Minerva
	Golden Arrow	Cygnus, Ibis, Minerva, Perseus, Phoenix
	Ocean Liner Expresses	Ibis, Ione, Zena
	Queen of Scots	Ione, Zena
	South Wales Pullman	Ione, Zena
	Talisman	Ione
	Tees-Tyne Pullman	Ione, Zena
	Torbay Pullman	Ione, Zena
	Yorkshire Pullman	Ione, Zena

ACKNOWLEDGMENTS

When I first went to Steamtown five years ago I knew absolutely nothing about trains or the Orient-Express. As I clambered in and out of derelict Pullmans with smashed windows and filthy marquetry I was secretly amazed that my husband felt something could be rescued from the mess. But during the restoration the vintage carriages regained their personalities and I became more and more intrigued by their different histories. I wanted to write the restoration story when I realized that very few passengers on the train had the slightest conception of the work involved in the restoration or knew anything about the fascinating historical background linking the Golden Arrow and the Simplon-Orient-Express.

As a complete novice in the railway world I was helped by many experts and enthusiasts. George Hinchcliffe, Director of Steamtown Museum, Ray Towell and Bob Timmins provided me with inform-ation on the British Pullmans and Bill McAlpine lent me his precious Pullman books. Mrs Albert Jones allowed me to photograph me-mentoes of her husband's Pullman service in charge of royal specials after the war, and David Lowther sent me the history of his car *Audrey* and checked my other Pullman material.

Paul Bianchini led me to the most useful archives in Paris, found posters and postcards and helped enormously with background material. The research for the continental coaches could hardly have started without George Behrend. His invaluable books were a constant source of reference and he was able to send many details of the history of individual cars. Mlle Agnes Sevestre did preliminary work in the Wagons-Lits archives and Mlle M. Bonnet and Mme C. Constantin were very helpful tracking down pictures there. I arrived at the offices of *La Vie du Rail* to find an array of useful articles already assembled – thanks to Mlle D. Brogeton. Gerard Maurois introduced me to the Travellers Club and the naughty stories of the Deauville Express, all at a splendid lunch. Mrs Beth Vinding wrote me a marvellous account of her family's ordeal marooned by snow in the Simplon-Orient-Express in 1929. Bob Dunn showed me how to make marquetry and allowed me to examine his father's records (which contained the original designs for some of our cars).

I particularly want to thank Pierre Fix-Masseau for doing the cover of this book amazingly fast and exactly in the way I had envisaged it. Chris Perkin took many of the photographs and kept track of lots more in his records for the VS-O-E.

I have been given all sorts of help and encouragement by Colin Bather, Bill Galvin, Claude Ginella, Billy Hamilton, Chris Holt, Adil Iskaros, Alan Pegler, Tony Poynder, Tim Robbins, Peter Rozee, Natale Rusconi, Maurizio Saccani, Theodora Simmons, Tony Spald-ing and Thelma Stevenson and many, many more connected with the VS-O-E project.

Weidenfeld & Nicolson provided a most skillful team to put the book together. Paul Atterbury helped me organise the manuscript, Julia Brown produced some fascinating pictures, Anne Dobell has been a most meticulous editor and Trevor Vincent has put the text and pictures together with great care.

Finally I would like to thank Peter Reid, who collated the information for the two maps of the routes of our coaches, did all the typing and kept track of innumerable pictures with unfailing good humour and enthusiasm, helped with the bibliography and compiled the index; Simon Sherwood, who chased almost all the continental pictures for me in Paris; and lastly, my husband, who has made so many constructive suggestions about every aspect of the book and introduced me to the wonderful world of railways.

Georges Nagelmackers

George Mortimer Pullman

André Noblemaire

Davidson Dalziel

James B. Sherwood

INTRODUCTION

The second question everyone asks about my involvement with the train is 'Were you a railway buff as a little boy?'. The answer is 'No, but I am now!'.

The first question is, of course, 'Why did you do it?'. The Sea Containers Group made its first venture into the luxury hotel business in 1976 by purchasing the renowned Cipriani Hotel in Venice. Sea Containers wanted to acquire other leisure properties in Europe but found that many of the best known were 'affairs of the heart' and not of the pocket. When the last trip of the Orient-Express took place in May 1977 the world-wide publicity was enormous; this was followed by a Sotheby's sale in Monte Carlo in October 1977 of five 1920s Orient-Express carriages which had been used in the film *Murder on the Orient Express*. I decided to attend the sale with the idea of picking up some bargains. The mob scene of press and TV which jammed the Monte Carlo railway goods depot that day convinced me that there was magic in the Orient-Express name. I bought two of the carriages and sent them to the Sea Containers depot in Bordeaux, France, where they were stored under cover for two years while the Venice Simplon-Orient-Express project was devised.

It took four and a half years from the date of the Monte Carlo sale to locate the rolling stock, learn how to restore it, negotiate the routing, engage the staff and promote the operation. The first run of the Venice Simplon-Orient-Express was on 25 May 1982 from London to Venice. I gave the inaugural speech standing on platform 8 at Victoria Station in front of Pullman coach *Audrey*, facing a battery of cameramen from all over the world.

THE MEN
BEHIND THE
VENICE SIMPLON-ORIENT-EXPRESS

Georges Nagelmackers,
founder of the Wagons-Lits Company and
originator of the Orient-Express in 1883.

James B. Sherwood,
originator of the
Venice Simplon-
Orient-Express.

André Noblemaire,
who organised the start of the
Simplon-Orient-Express in 1919.
He was Director-General of the
Wagons-Lits Company.

George Mortimer Pullman,
creator of the Pullman Car Company
and initiator of luxury train travel in
the USA in the mid-nineteenth century.

Davidson Dalziel,
who started the Golden Arrow and the Flèche d'Or
all-Pullman service from London to Paris in 1926.
He owned the British Pullman Car Company
and was on the board of Wagons-Lits.

'I know just how the Pope feels. Both he and I are committed to inaugural events in Britain this week and we are both wondering whether they are appropriate in view of the Falklands war. Nevertheless, we are going ahead with the inaugural of the Venice Simplon-Orient-Express because thousands of people have been working on these fabulous, historic Pullman and Orient-Express trains over the last four and a half years and their efforts deserve to be recognised. And 15,000 passengers are waiting their turn to travel on them.

One hundred years ago, almost to this very day, the first Pullman car was introduced into a continental boat train. The car was called *Jupiter*. It left from Victoria Station, probably only a few feet from where we are standing, and it operated to Dover on the line of the London, Chatham & Dover Railway. The Pullman car was an American idea, that of George Mortimer Pullman, and *Jupiter* had been assembled in Derby in 1875 from parts supplied by Pullman from America. Unfortunately *Jupiter* was not a financial success because the prospective passengers did not want to pay the supplement on the fare to ride in her. I trust we will have no repetition of that sort of thing.

We are almost upon the centenary of the Orient-Express. It started in 1883 as a service from Paris to Constantinople proceeding north of the Alps. The most famous of the Orient-Express trains was the Simplon-Orient-Express and it came into being in a rather unusual way, by international treaty, the Treaty of Versailles in 1919. The service was dictated by articles 321–386 and the routing from Paris via Lausanne, Milan and Venice was required by the Western powers in order to avoid any dependence upon Germany and Austria, as these countries were deeply distrusted. The first Simplon-Orient-Express trip took place on 15 April 1919 and the last on 27 May 1977. The last trip of the by then decrepit train generated so much interest throughout the world that I made a mental note to investigate whether the train could be revived in all its between-the-wars glory. Today we see the result of that investigation.

The Orient-Express perhaps had the intrigue and the glory but Britons were carried to the Orient-Express in lush Pullmans in which many of you are going to ride today. The oldest car in our rake is *Ibis*, built in 1925 by the Birmingham Railway Carriage and Wagon Company. It operated in France and Italy in its early years, then spent much of its life running in the Golden Arrow service from Victoria to Dover and Folkestone. It is one of my favourite cars because the marquetry panels squeak as the carriage leans into turns. I was not allowed to ride in her today because the TV people said it squeaks too much for their sound recorders.

Our ceremony today is being held in front of *Audrey*, built in 1932 by the Metropolitan Cammell Carriage and Wagon Company Limited for the Southern Belle, the world's first motorised Pullman service, which operated from London to Brighton starting in 1933. In 1934 the Pullman Car Company changed the name of the service to the Brighton Belle and I think this service was one of the best known and loved in the country. *Audrey*'s marquetry does not squeak.

Before I cut the ribbon I want to thank a few of the people who have been instrumental in bringing back this Pullman train: Lord Garnock and General Gribbon of Sallingbury, Bill McAlpine who made Steamtown in Carnforth available to us for the restoration, George Hinchcliffe and George Walker at Steamtown who carried out the work, Jack Bedser and James Mackay of British Rail who have been so helpful and patient with us novices in the railway business, and Alan Branch at Sealink who will be getting us across the Channel in comfort and on time. I also want to thank Sir Peter and Lady Parker for joining us today and express to him our hope that the current tensions between the unions and management of British Rail will be relieved so that our train and all the others can operate with regularity in the future.

It has been a great effort. It cost £11 million to restore the Pullman and Orient-Express trains and I hope you will agree we have a grand result. I now declare the Venice Simplon-Orient-Express resumed.'

J B Sherwood

*James Sherwood at Victoria Station on 25 May 1982 giving his speech
before the inaugural run of the Venice Simplon-Orient-Express,
standing in front of Pullman* Audrey.

[13]

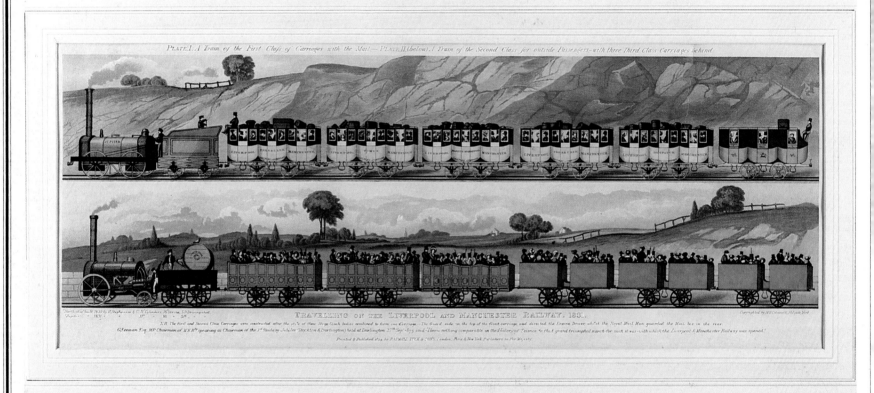

Nineteenth-century engraving showing the Liverpool and Manchester Railway in 1831.
The upper train is made up of first-class carriages, while the lower illustrates the
lack of protection offered to second and third-class travellers at that time.
This engraving can be seen in Pullman Cygnus.

Chapter One

THE HISTORY OF THE ORIENT-EXPRESS

IT all started with the American George Mortimer Pullman. He was the first to visualise the possibilities of luxury train travel when he built the *Pioneer* in 1864, the first railway carriage designed with true comfort for the passenger. Railway innovators from both England and the Continent were impressed by his achievements and were inspired to follow his lead in introducing similar standards in their cars (at that time the American railway system was far in advance of anything in Europe). Pullman was invited to England by James Allport, General Manager of the Midland Railway, and this visit eventually led to the formation of the Pullman Palace Car Company in 1882. From that time onwards luxury train travel in Britain was dominated by this firm.

Pullman also tried to infiltrate European luxury train travel. But Georges Nagelmackers, who founded the Wagons-Lits Company in 1876, had created a virtual monopoly on the Continent with his luxury trains forming a connecting network of services across Europe. The Orient-Express was the most famous of these international expresses. Nagelmackers in turn also attempted to penetrate the British market, but he never captured any significant part of it. So today the Venice Simplon-Orient-Express consists of two trains. The English rake which takes passengers from Victoria to Folkestone is composed of chocolate and cream coloured Pullman parlour cars, most of which have been part of the Golden Arrow. In contrast, the continental rake is composed of restaurant and sleeping cars drawn from the grand international Trains de Luxe which crossed Europe between the wars – particularly rolling stock used in the Simplon-Orient-Express at its most glamorous period. This train bears the distinctive dark blue livery and golden-brass lettering of the Compagnie Internationale des Wagons-Lits et des Grands Express Européens.

There are really two stories to be traced in the background of the VS-O-E. One is that of the Orient-Express itself and particularly of its most opulent offspring, the Simplon-Orient-Express. The other is the development of luxury train services between London and Paris, cities separated by the awkward gap of the English Channel; these services culminated in the Golden Arrow and its French counterpart, the Flèche d'Or.

THE DEVELOPMENT OF LUXURY RAIL TRAVEL
BETWEEN LONDON AND PARIS

Early in the nineteenth century there were dozens of small railway companies ramifying all over Britain and the Continent, often competing in a ridiculous fashion. The rolling stock was extremely basic. Luxury was a cover on top of the railway carriage and a seat to sit on (an Act of Parliament made this compulsory in 1844). Crossing the Channel was complicated by the large tidal differences and the rudimentary harbours. The hardy traveller put to sea in a little rowing boat and was transferred to a larger vessel standing out in the harbour. The constantly changing train departures from London reflected the problems of a tide-dependent service. Later, harbour piers were built and extended, allowing small shallow-draft paddle steamers to tie up. The harbours of Dover, Folkestone, Boulogne and Calais were finally dredged, railway lines were built through onto the piers and it became possible to berth larger and more stable ships. By 1903 the paddle steamer was beginning to be replaced by turbine engine ferries of deeper draft.

In the 1840s the railway companies needed the accolade of royal approval for people to regard them as safe for passengers as well as freight. Prince Albert had travelled by train when courting Queen Victoria but she did not risk her royal person until 1842 when she journeyed from Slough to London, with the famous engineer Isam-

Queen Victoria crosses the new Tay Bridge on 5 July 1879. The bridge collapsed during a storm only five months later while a train was going over it.

RIGHT *Queen Victoria's saloon, built in 1869 by the London and North Western Railway.*

Painting by Howard Geach showing a South Eastern Railway boat train leaving a stormy Dover harbour, c. 1865.

bard Kingdom Brunel driving the engine. There was some criticism of this daring feat (railways were considered far too dangerous for so illustrious a personage) but she enjoyed the trip and confounded her critics by making the return journey with the infant Albert Edward, Prince of Wales. Just about as much furore was caused recently by the present Prince of Wales when he travelled *en famille* with his wife and their new baby, Prince William, on a flight to Scotland.

There were in fact a number of bad accidents in the early days of the railways as the coaches were flimsy, the couplings poor and the brakes often woefully inadequate. Gradually, improvements were made in brakes, bogies and carriages. These later contributed to the success of Pullman and Wagons-Lits cars, as their well-constructed carriages survived many accidents in which other types collapsed and crumpled.

James Allport had been tremendously impressed by Pullman and had travelled many miles in his coaches in America. He invited Pullman to meet the Midland Railway shareholders in Britain, who agreed that Pullman could build coaches in Illinois, ship them to Britain and operate them on the Midland Railway for a supplement over the normal train fare. By 1874 the coaches *Midland* and *Excelsior* had been built, shipped and reassembled at the Midland Railway workshops in Derby. These first two sleeping cars joined *Victoria*, the first English parlour car, for a trial run to Bedford and during the journey the first meal was served on an English train. Late in 1881 the Pullman Limited Express became the first all-Pullman train in Europe running from London to Brighton. It was also the first train to be lit by electricity, supplied by batteries slung under the floor of *Beatrice*. The

batteries were charged by a special dynamo driven by a steam engine installed on the platform at Victoria. Because the service also ran on Sundays it became known as the 'Sabbath Breaker'. It was renamed the Brighton Belle in 1934 (Pullman *Audrey* in the VS-O-E was built for the Brighton Belle).

In 1882 the Pullman Palace Car Company was registered in England. The parlour car *Jupiter*, assembled earlier for the Midland Railway, became the first Pullman running in a boat train called the Dover Continental Pullman Car Boat Express. The service ran for only two years as there was considerable customer resistance to paying the surcharge.

The next attempt at luxury boat train services, the Club Trains, lasted about five years. In 1889 it was fashionable to go over to France for the Paris Exhibition, taking the Club Train from London to

Dover, crossing the Channel in a specially commissioned ferry and connecting with a luxury service from Calais to Paris. There were actually two Club Trains, run by rival railway companies, composed of two sets of six identical Wagons-Lits saloons painted olive green with bronze crests. They both left London at about the same time and raced for Dover where the local railway buffs took bets on which would arrive first. A contemporary poster advertises the Club Train as the start of the Orient-Express service running to Constantinople. It also announces that no passports would be required for the whole journey. The Club Trains were forerunners of the Golden Arrow and the Flèche d'Or and they connected with the main Orient-Express rake in Paris in a similar way. They were withdrawn in 1893, as both rival railway companies had made substantial losses on the services. They failed because of reluctance to pay the surcharge, political tensions between France and England, and perhaps also because they were not very well advertised (Bradshaw's Railway Guide did not appear until a couple of years later). This was Wagons-Lits' only real attempt to compete with Pullman in England before World War I.

Although not strictly a boat train, the Folkestone Vestibule was an interesting luxury train to the Channel port. Built in 1897 in Birmingham for the South Eastern Railway, the cars offered such luxuries as electric lighting, heating and linked gangways. The first-class cars had interiors of Italian walnut, Louis Quinze decoration, Axminster carpets and separate ladies' and gentlemen's lavatories.

In 1908 the British Pullman Company was bought by Sir Davidson Dalziel, who started building Pullman cars in England rather than having them shipped in pieces from the USA. He also bought the right to use the name 'Pullman' which had become synonymous with luxury train travel. The company went public in 1915 and Dalziel remained chairman and the largest shareholder. He formed an interesting link with the Wagons-Lits Company as he became one of their directors and his daughter married René Nagelmackers (the son of Georges). In 1926 he became chairman of the Wagons-Lits Share Trust, which gave him a controlling interest in Wagons-Lits.

By 1913 there were five daily boat trains in each direction including eleven Pullman coaches with evocative names like *Valencia*, *Florence* and *Clementina*. Both the English and French boat trains generally contained restaurant cars, such as *Shamrock* in the Flushing Pullman Restaurant Car Night Mail. The time from London to Paris via Dover and Calais was reduced to six and a half hours, which has not been

Poster advertising the short-lived London-Paris Club Train services. Established in 1889, these were the first all-Pullman trains to link the two capitals.

OPPOSITE
Nineteenth-century print showing the Shakespeare Viaduct and Tunnel near Dover. This print is in Pullman Perseus.

*The Golden Arrow leaving London's Victoria Station on its way to Dover in 1947,
hauled by a Southern Railway locomotive.*

[20]

bettered since, despite improved ferries and electrification of the lines.

The outbreak of World War I in August 1914 put an end to all civilian travel across the Channel; Dover and Folkestone became troop embarkation ports. After the war Dover and Boulogne were the first harbours to re-open but the rail connections across Europe were complicated because the Nord Railway had to carry out extensive repair work wherever its tracks passed through the battlefields of northern France. The boat trains started again despite these difficulties and by 1924 there was an all-Pullman service from Victoria to Dover. Two years later the Flèche d'Or was inaugurated between Calais and Paris and connected with the English Pullman service with Lord Dalziel's enthusiastic support. It was composed of ten new first-class Pullmans with marquetry interiors and body shells of steel painted in the Pullman 'chocolate and cream' livery. This prestigious train was matched in 1929 by the Golden Arrow Limited which connected with its own cross-Channel steamer, the *Canterbury*. The services were distinguished by large arrows on the engines and also on the sides of the coaches. It was quite the smartest, most fashionable way to cross the Channel. Passengers who wished to connect with the Simplon-Orient-Express joined a through Wagons-Lits sleeping car attached to the Flèche d'Or at Calais and when they got to Paris they were shunted round the Petite Ceinture to the Gare de Lyon, where their sleeper was connected to the main rake of the S-O-E. One of the English Pullmans in the VS-O-E, *Ibis*, was part of the Golden Arrow from 1930 onwards.

The twenties and early thirties were the heyday of luxury train travel. The carriages built in that period were the most comfortable, elegant and luxurious ever constructed. They were decorated by the best designers and had elaborate plush and the loveliest marquetry interiors. It was the grand way to travel across to France and on to Istanbul, with superb service, elaborate meals and glamorous companions. Yet it did not last for long. The Depression reduced the number of first-class passengers and consequently the number of Pullmans used in the Golden Arrow and Flèche d'Or. Gradually second-class Pullmans or even ordinary first-class cars were added to the services.

In 1936 the inauguration of the Night Ferry provided another way to reach Paris from London. Twenty sleepers were specially constructed by Wagons-Lits so that they could be transferred across the Channel by custom-built train-ferries from France into England and

Lord Dalziel, chairman of the Pullman Car Company, with one of the new generation of Pullman cars built in England for the Wagons-Lits Company in 1927 for the Flèche d'Or.

The Golden Arrow motif being removed from the locomotive after the last steam-hauled run of the Pullman Express from Dover to Victoria Station on 11 June 1961. The service finally closed in 1972.

*Poster produced by Wagons-Lits to advertise
the new Golden Arrow London–Paris Pullman service,
inaugurated in 1926. The artist was W. S. Bylitiphs.*

so it became possible for the first time to travel between the two cities without leaving the train. This route became a favourite of the Duke of Windsor and others who wanted to be carried discreetly across the Channel while still asleep. This very successful service was the only one that transported the passenger coaches across the Channel by ferry. It eventually ended in 1980.

On the night of 30 September 1939, the start of World War II, the Night Ferry and Golden Arrow stopped operating. Luxury travel ceased and Pullman saloons became stationary restaurant cars or troop canteens or were stored for the duration. At the outbreak of war the Pullman Car Company owned about 200 cars in Britain; during the course of the war half were damaged and four completely destroyed. *Audrey* was damaged in an air raid at Victoria Station and when she was restored for the VS-O-E shrapnel splinters were dug out of the marquetry panels. All the Pullman records were lost in the bombing of 1944. The Southern Railway lost twelve ships, but the *Canterbury* survived Dunkirk and action on the Normandy beaches, carrying in assault craft. By the end of the war Calais and Boulogne were almost completely obliterated and the harbours had to be extensively rebuilt.

The Simplon-Orient-Express resumed in January 1946, from Paris to Milan, Venice and Rome. In April the Golden Arrow and Flèche d'Or started again, connected by a renovated *Canterbury*, and through sleeping cars from Calais were attached to the S-O-E by May 1946.

The gradual run-down of luxury train services after the war was triggered by the cheapness of air travel compared with rail journeys, especially those with the Pullman surcharge. People lost the habit of taking the train for long journeys and expected the speed and economy of air travel.

Gradually electrification of tracks spread across Britain and Europe. In 1961 the last steam-hauled journey of the Golden Arrow took place. In 1963 the Pullman Car Company, which had not been nationalised with British Rail in 1954, was merged with British Transport Hotels, and later the Company's works at Preston Park, near Brighton, were closed down. In 1969 Pullman Cars were withdrawn from the Flèche d'Or and in 1972 the Golden Arrow service was ended. The final journey included *Phoenix*, *Perseus*, *Cygnus* and *Carina*.

THE EVOLUTION OF THE ORIENT-EXPRESSES

On the Continent the problems of establishing luxury train services to the East were caused by the passage from country to country rather than the crossing of the Channel. Over the years the European services have been dictated by shifting borders, wars, the new requirements of middle-class travellers, the needs of colonists to get to their colonies and for the mail to get through to far-flung outposts of empire, by the Russian Revolution, the Iron Curtain and by the arrival of relatively cheap air travel and competition from the motor car.

During the first half of the nineteenth century every country in Europe was busy building its own railway system independently of those of its neighbours. There was a positive desire to have incompatible rolling-stock and track in case of invasion. The transcontinental traveller usually went by ship or stage coach and if he was brave enough to face the rigours of train travel he had to change onto a different railway system at every border he crossed. The public railway coach was modified from the horse-drawn carriage: it had four to six wheels (no bogies), no lavatories, no restaurant or bar cars, no corridors, no vestibules or connections between coaches, often no springing, hard seats, rudimentary heating and virtually no lighting. It was not comfortable.

Georges Nagelmackers, creator of the Orient-Express, had the almost visionary idea of changing the whole concept of through-railway travel across Europe. He was born at Liège in Belgium on 24 June 1845, the son of a wealthy father who was already involved in the development of the Belgian railway system. The family were bankers for Leopold II, King of the Belgians, who proved an important contact later on when Nagelmackers was dealing with foreign courts.

In 1869 Nagelmackers visited America to recover from a broken heart. (It was said that he had fallen in love with his cousin – either the family did not approve or he was spurned.) He may have met George Mortimer Pullman at that time and he certainly admired his luxurious railway cars with seats that could be adapted into bunks for overnight travel. Passengers paid a supplement to travel in these cars and Pullman organised contracts with the railways so that they could be attached to trains and pulled across each state.

Fired with enthusiasm, Nagelmackers returned to Belgium, determined to form an international company to run luxurious coaches on well-planned routes right across Europe, passing national frontiers, a revolutionary concept at the time. He ordered the first five sleeping

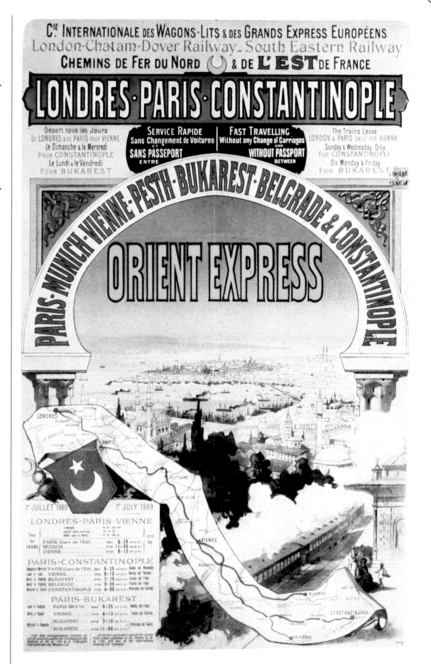

Poster advertising the Orient-Express, giving details of the route between London and Constantinople and the timetable for services during the summer of 1889.

Mann Boudoir Sleeping Car of 1873. Colonel Mann is seated on the running board,
with Georges Nagelmackers standing beside him.

cars ever built in Europe to be constructed in Vienna. He reached agreement with the French and German railway authorities – but at the onset of the Franco-Prussian War in 1870 it looked as if all his efforts would be frustrated. However, as a Belgian, he was able to by-pass the war to some extent and began more negotiations in Italy to develop a service from Ostend to Brindisi, which at that time was the starting point of many shipping routes to the East. But again he ran into trouble: with the opening of the Mont Cenis tunnel through the Alps in 1871, his own longer route over the Brenner Pass became much

less attractive and he soon lost his passengers and valuable mail contract to the faster route. Eventually he ran his first sleeping cars between Ostend and Berlin, Paris and Cologne, and Vienna and Munich in 1872.

He ordered another set of five cars, this time six-wheelers, to be built in Germany. These were used on the Paris to Vienna route which turned out to be his first profitable service, and whose success provided him with the evidence he so urgently needed to sell his luxury approach to the railway companies and his backers.

Early in 1873 Nagelmackers found himself in somewhat straitened circumstances, and in order to expand his financial base he formed a partnership with Colonel William d'Alton Mann, an American entrepreneur who had recently moved to London. They formed a short-lived company called Mann's Railway Sleeping Car Company Limited.

Mann was a colourful character who had been an oil prospector, tax collector and newspaper proprietor, and the owner of an influential and inventive scandal sheet. More important, he had developed a luxury railway carriage in America and although he was no real competitor to Pullman there, he did make the first attempt to bring luxury coaches to England in the form of 'Mann's Boudoir Cars'.

Over the next few years Nagelmackers, with financial backing from London and the help of his important contacts in the Belgian court, succeeded in forming a valuable series of interlocking contracts on the Continent, thwarting Pullman's attempt in 1874 to set up a European network. He was assisted in this by King Leopold II, a notoriously mean railway enthusiast, who was connected by family ties with most of the crowned heads of Europe and liked to travel by train to visit them. Leopold realised that he could travel free if he helped the infant Wagons-Lits Company obtain those vital contracts with foreign courts. His enthusiasm and influence paved the way for Nagelmackers to clinch deals with the many countries between Paris and Constantinople. Leopold always travelled in the company of the prettiest ladies. While he was enamoured of the dancer Cleo de Merode he became known as 'King Cleopold' and contemporary cartoons show him *en train* with her. In 1876 Nagelmackers bought out the dubious Colonel Mann and became the owner of their joint collection of fifty-three Mann's Boudoir cars. In December of that year he formed the present Compagnie Internationale des Wagons-Lits with King Leopold II heading the list of patrons. At that time he had eighteen firm contracts and three trial contracts on various railway systems across Europe.

Colonel Mann returned to the USA in a further attempt to compete with Pullman on his home ground, but in the late 1880s Mann's American company was bought up by Pullman.

Nagelmackers produced increasingly comfortable cars and the services were extended through many new countries. The first European-built bogie sleeping car (75) was tried out on various routes in 1880 but was not universally accepted as safe, although bogie sleeping cars became acceptable in 1883 (bogies allow the wheels to swivel independently of the carriage, giving a smoother ride round bends). Nagelmackers reconstructed a carriage to form a rudimentary dining car with tables and chairs where passengers could sit to eat their own food, as meals were still not provided on trains.

In 1881 the first custom-built restaurant car in Europe was built in Munich. Car 107 had walls padded in Spanish leather and ceilings painted in an Italian stucco design. The kitchen was placed between two saloons, which each contained twelve chairs. The stove was coal-fired and there was also cold storage space in a pantry. The real significance of the kitchen-restaurant car was that long-distance trains were no longer forced to stop at small stations for the passengers to forage at station buffets – and thus the time of the journey could be reduced. The food and wine provided were also of a higher quality than those found at remote stations – and passengers were prepared to pay for this quality and convenience.

In 1882 the first train composed solely of Wagons-Lits coaches was

English postcard showing the Orient-Express near Constantinople.

displayed at the Gare de l'Est in Paris before leaving for Vienna. It included restaurant car 107 as well as the sleeping car 75 used for the bogie trials and some other sleepers. The journey to Vienna took twenty-eight hours – about four hours less than usual. This suggested that, using similar rolling stock, the trip to Constantinople could be shortened by a day and a half.

Nagelmackers became involved in extended negotiations for the Orient-Express route. He organised a conference in Constantinople early in 1883 with representatives from eight railway companies. It was agreed that the Express d'Orient should be made up of two luggage vans (one for mail), one restaurant car and two or more sleeping cars. It started running, but without official inauguration, on 5 June 1883, from Paris to Vienna.

The official inauguration was held at last on 4 October 1883, a famous occasion in railway history. By that time Wagons-Lits had taken delivery of five new bogie sleeping cars and the first bogie restaurant car. The route was from Paris through Strasbourg, Vienna, Budapest, Bucharest and Giurgi on the Danube in Romania. At this point, the passengers left the new cars and crossed the river by ferry to Rustchuk. There they boarded old rolling stock provided by the Austrian Eastern Railway which provided a striking contrast to the Wagons-Lits coaches. They left this train at Varna to board the *Espero* for a rather rough eighteen-hour sea voyage to Constantinople. The journey usually took four days (*see map, p. 6–7*).

There were glowing accounts of this memorable inauguration. A smart crowd of Parisians gathered at the Gare de l'Est to admire the gleaming train of varnished teak carriages pulled by an outside cylinder Est 2–4–0 engine. For the first time the cars had the full title of Compagnie Internationale des Wagons-Lits et des Grands Express Européens displayed along their sides. It was the start of the most famous Grand Express service of all time.

The passengers were French, Belgian, German, Turkish and Austrian, and included Opper de Blowitz representing *The Times* and another well known author, Edmond About, who eventually wrote a complete book about the journey. They found the luxuriously appointed cars much more comfortable than the earlier six-wheelers as the bogies made the ride far smoother. Nagelmackers had spared no effort to ensure the success of this much-publicised trip, providing beautiful crystal and linen, elaborate food, excellent wine and impeccable service. The sleeping cars converted from their night-time configur-

Sleeping car in the Orient-Express. The compartments are shown in their day and night-time configurations. There was a lavatory and washbasin to each carriage.

The restaurant car in the Orient-Express in 1883.

ation of two bunks per compartment to comfortable benches in the day time. Each sleeping car had bunks for twenty passengers and two washbasins with lavatories. Even soap was provided – an unusual luxury for that period.

During the trip a number of *divertissements* were provided to entertain the passengers. There were official welcomes at Strasbourg, Vienna and Budapest. Hungarian minstrels boarded the train at Szwgedin, played vigorously for more than two hours and finished with the *Marseillaise*, with the chef singing a vociferous solo. The passengers were received by King Charles of Hohenzollern at his new Summer Palace at Peles. De Blowitz managed to arrange an exclusive interview with him, which he later glowingly recounted in *The Times*.

After the euphoria of the inaugural trip the Express d'Orient settled into a regular routine. By 1884 it had become a daily service as far as Budapest and by 1885 there were various alternative routings at the eastern end of the run. In 1889 the railway track was completed all the way through from Paris to Constantinople, the journey taking 67 hours 35 minutes. It became an important vehicle for the mail as well as for passengers.

At the end of the nineteenth century Wagons-Lits began providing hotels at strategically important places on the journey to cater for the growing number of tourists. In Constantinople they built the Bosphorus Summer Palace Hotel overlooking the Straits into Asia and the Pera Palace. In 1903 they acquired a health resort at Tatra-Lomnicz from the Hungarian Government. This had originally been the Emperor's Palace and was built 8,000 feet up in the Carpathian Mountains. It had an extensive winter sports programme of sledging, wild turkey shooting, skiing and skating. In its brochure it claimed to be equipped with 'Hockey, Pigging and Tennis Apparatus'.

People often think that the Orient-Express was just one train that ran on one route, from Paris to Constantinople. In fact there were several different services over different routes to the East and a number of destinations in addition to Constantinople. This extension of luxury services to Eastern Europe took place during the late nineteenth and early twentieth centuries and the routes continued to change with the building of bridges, the shifting of frontiers and the extension of railway lines into the more remote parts of the East. Travellers from Britain joined the transcontinental trains at Ostend for the eastern route connecting through to Warsaw, Vienna and Bucharest, and from Calais via Paris and Venice to Constantinople.

Poster advertising the Simplon-Orient-Express route to Constantinople by promoting the attractions of Venice.

The Paris-Constantinople line divided at Belgrade with one section continuing through to Athens.

By the turn of the century new sleeping cars had been modified with all-steel bogies, enclosed vestibules and concertina gangways between the cars. There were generally eighteen berths per car and most compartments had built-in washbasins and commodes. By the end of the century Wagons-Lits had opened various workshops to service their carriages. One of them was at Slykens, near Ostend, which is where most of the VS-O-E sleeping cars were restored.

In 1905 Georges Nagelmackers died at his country home at Villepreux-les-Clayes, but not before he had seen the 1000th Wagon-Lit and dining car 999 shown at the International Exhibition at Liège. His great vision and drive had established 'Madame La Compagnie', as Wagons-Lits was affectionately called, as an international entity with services stretching beyond the confines of Europe, and with a great tradition of service and luxury.

The next important development in the VS-O-E history was the building of the twelve-mile-long Simplon Tunnel through the Alps between Brig and Domodossola. This great engineering feat was started in 1898, and the tunnel opened in 1906.

As soon as it was opened the Simplon Express started to run on the route used by the VS-O-E today, from Paris through Lausanne, Brig, the Simplon Tunnel, Milan and on to Venice. Construction also started in 1906 on the enormous railway station in Milan. By 1912 the Simplon Express terminated in Trieste – it went no further because Trieste was at that time part of Austria, and the Austrian railway authorities refused to allow the passage of international trains through the country if they did not pass through Vienna.

With the declaration of war in 1914 all the various services of the Orient-Express were halted in France, Austria, Serbia and Turkey and the Wagons-Lits office was forced to move to Paris (where it has remained ever since), as Brussels was occupied by the Germans.

In 1916 the German Railway Company Mitropa was formed, using sequestered Wagons-Lits rolling stock that had been trapped in Germany. But Wagons-Lits' biggest loss occurred in 1919, as a result of events following the Russian Revolution. (Nagelmackers had established a route into Russia by 1887 to St Petersburg, and from 1908 Wagons-Lits operated all the Trains de Luxe on the Trans-Siberian railway.) Wagons-Lits lost 161 coaches without compensation and had to withdraw all their staff.

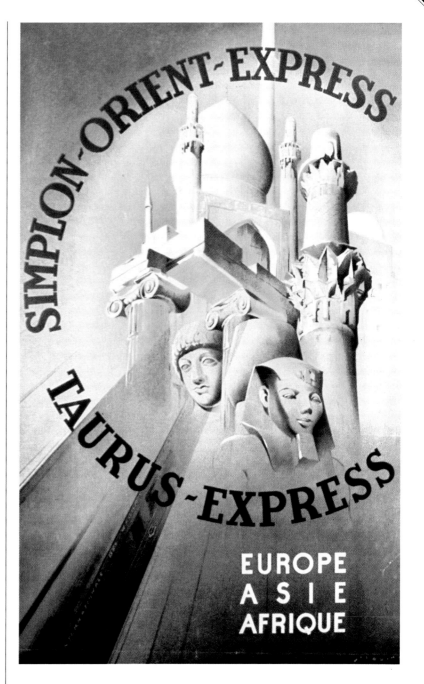

Poster advertising the Simplon-Orient-Express and the Taurus Express.

LEFT *On 11 November 1918 Marshal Foch, seated in the centre of the photograph, received the German surrender in Wagons-Lits dining car 2419. The car had been shunted onto a siding in the Forest of Compiègne, twenty-five miles north east of Paris.*

ABOVE *On 22 June 1940 car 2419 was hauled back to precisely the same spot in the Forest of Compiègne for Hitler to receive the surrender of France.*

The Armistice was signed on 11 November 1918. It was witnessed by Marshal Foch at Compiègne near Réthondes in the most historic Wagons-Lits car of all time, 2419. (This car was later dragged from its museum by Hitler's troops to receive the surrender of the French in 1940 in exactly the same place as the World War I Armistice had been signed. Hitler then had the symbolic car removed to Berlin. It was eventually blown up by an SS unit just before the German capitulation in 1945, to prevent a humiliating repetition of history.)

At the end of World War I the Allies laid down routes for the major train services in the Treaty of Versailles. Articles 321 to 386, which were principally concerned with international waterways and the new republic of Czechoslovakia, also dealt with the future of international rail transport. The Allies wanted to create speedy communications between the West and the new Baltic countries, avoiding Germany and Austria. They ordered an international route to be opened via Italy, through the newly created country of Yugoslavia and on to

SIMPLON
ORIENT
EXPRESS:
TAURUS
EXPRESS.

ANNEES 1930·1931.

ET LEURS BRANCHES CORRESPONDANTES

Echelle 1 : 10.000.000ème

OSLO
STOCKHOLM
RIGA
DUBLIN
KJØBENHAVN
KAUNAS
LONDON
Amsterdam
DEN HAAG
Dover
Ostende
Calais
BRUXELLES
BERLIN
WARSZAWA
Köln
Dresden
Breslau
Francfort a/m
Karlovy.Vary
PARIS
PRAHA
Dijon
BERNE
Lausanne
Simplon
Bratislava
Galanta
Lyon
WIEN
Milano
BUDAPEST
Bordeaux
Torino
Venezia
Trieste
Soubotica
Zagreb
Timisoara
MADRID
Vinkovci
BEOGRAD
BUCURESTI
Orsova
Nich
MER NOIRE
ROMA
SOFIA
Istanbul
Haydarpaşa
ALGER
Salonique
Eskişehir
ANKARA
TUNIS
Adana
Mardine
Nissibin
Mossoul
ATHÈNES
Alep
Kirkuk
Homs
Tripoli
Rayak
BAGDAD
Beyrouth
DAMAS
Hilla
Haifa
Ur
TRIPOLI
JERUSALEM
Kantara
Bassorah
CAIRO

MER DU NORD
MANCHE
ATLANTIQUE
MER
MÉDITERRANÉE

Simplon-Orient-Express.
d°   Branches correspondantes.
Taurus-Express.
Lignes adjacentes
Services automobiles.

Map published by the Wagons-Lits Company for the season 1930–1, showing the routes of the Simplon-Orient-Express and the Taurus Express.

The Simplon-Orient-Express at the Turkish frontier.

Constantinople. The Simplon-Orient-Express was inaugurated on 11 April 1919, routed from Paris via Dijon, Lausanne, the Simplon Tunnel, Milan, Venice, Trieste, Zagreb, Belgrade, Nish and Sophia to Constantinople (the journey took fifty-six hours). There were through sleepers to Bucharest (detached at Vinkovci) and to Athens via Thessalonika (detached at Belgrade) along a newly completed line built during the Macedonian campaign. This service was organised by André Noblemaire, the Director General of the French Paris-Lyon-Méditerranée Railway. The Simplon-Orient-Express became the most famous and successful luxury express between the wars.

During the 1920s Wagons-Lits built their most luxurious fleet of coaches. All the continental coaches in the VS-O-E were built in this period. Some of these cars immediately went into service on the Simplon-Orient-Express, while others became part of other luxury expresses across Europe, particularly the famous *Train Bleu*. But the Depression began to affect the most expensive end of the travel market and some of the luxury expresses were reduced in length, although a few new routes such as the Arlberg-Orient-Express were initiated at this time. Passengers could join this train at Calais or Paris, then go through to Zürich, Vienna, Budapest and Bucharest.

The Anschluss of Austria in 1938 resulted in the breaking of all Wagons-Lits contracts there, and Mitropa took over their services in both Austria and Czechoslovakia. With the outbreak of World War II in September 1939 the Orient-Express and the Arlberg-Orient were immediately suspended. Curiously enough the Simplon-Orient continued to run until 1940, as it passed through Italy, which was still neutral, while sleeping cars from Berlin continued to join the train at Belgrade. French passengers were warned to be discreet in the German cars. During the war most of the Wagons-Lits coaches were requisitioned for troop accommodation, becoming stationary restaurants or even brothels. At the end of the war, Wagons-Lits had lost 845 cars, bombed, looted and sabotaged. But gradually camouflaged rolling stock was retrieved from all over Europe to be repaired in the Wagons-Lits workshops.

The Simplon-Orient-Express started up again in January 1946. It went from Paris to Istanbul but not to Athens as the Yugoslav-Greek border was closed because Greek Macedonia was occupied by the British and the Salonika-Athens line was inoperable due to Communist guerrilla activity. The Arlberg-Orient and the Orient-Express started again and ran a variety of trains ending in Prague, Warsaw, Bucharest or Belgrade. But from 1947 onwards the Iron Curtain isolating Communist Europe curtailed the Orient-Express routes.

The first services affected by the Iron Curtain were internal Wagons-Lits services in Yugoslavia which were taken over at the end of 1947; this was followed by the cessation of internal services in Romania in 1948. Wagons-Lits stopped operating in Hungary in 1949 and in Bulgaria and Czechoslovakia by 1950. In 1951 the Turkish border was closed and the Simplon-Orient terminated at Sofia or Svilengrad. However it was still possible to get to Turkey or Athens as the Greek-Yugoslav border had reopened that year and passengers changed at Salonika. The line from there into Turkey was so dangerous because of attacks by Communist bandits that the connection was only attempted in daylight. It became possible to through-run from Paris to Istanbul via Salonika again in 1952.

But these services were mere shadows of their former selves. The Orient-Express became so attenuated that it often consisted only of a single car tacked onto a local train. Sleepers ran without accompanying

The last run of the Direct-Orient-Express left Paris for Istanbul on the evening of 19 May 1977. The publicity surrounding this event encouraged James Sherwood to restore the service.

restaurant cars and the glamorous passengers of the golden days transferred their patronage to the airlines, which were now both faster and cheaper. As the services closed down, one by one, many of the luxury cars which are now in the VS-O-E were transferred to the Spanish and Portuguese railways where they ran until the 1970s.

The last run of the Orient-Express left Paris on 19 May 1977 from the Gare de Lyon. It was made up of a shabby sleeping car and three scruffy day coaches. There was no restaurant car and the passengers had to bring their own food or snatch what they could from station buffets en route. The train arrived in Istanbul over five hours late.

But the last run did not go unnoticed. There was an amazing response in the world press and this was followed by even more publicity when five Orient-Express cars were sold at Monte Carlo in October 1977. The two sleepers bought by James Sherwood, President of the Sea Containers Group, formed the nucleus of the Venice Simplon-Orient-Express rolling stock.

Chapter Two

THE STORIES OF THE CARRIAGES

I have written the history of each of the cars now running in the Venice Simplon-Orient-Express in considerable detail, quite deliberately. I felt that passengers on the train might like to look up 'their' car, to trace its routes and adventures. Every car can be identified by a plaque in its vestibule. The many different routes that the cars travelled are shown in two maps (pages 6–7 and 8) and details such as the date built, place of origin and distinguishing features of each coach are summarised in the table (page 73).

THE BRITISH PULLMANS

When the passengers for the Venice Simplon-Orient-Express arrive at Victoria Station in London, they find awaiting them a train composed of chocolate and cream Pullman parlour cars, each bearing proudly the insignia of the Pullman Car Company and its own name – *Audrey*, *Cygnus*, *Ibis*, *Ione*, *Minerva*, *Perseus*, *Phoenix* and *Zena*. These names evoke another age. The first Pullman cars which went into service in Britain in 1874 carried their names on their sides and this became a tradition. When the British carriages for the Venice Simplon-Orient-Express were rescued from railway sidings in Britain and France and brought to the workshops for restoration, their names were naturally restored as well. Sometimes the name emerged from under layers of paint.

Even though the Pullman Car Company records were destroyed during a bombing raid in 1944, it has proved possible to trace the life stories of all the carriages that make up the VS-O-E Pullman train,

with material from railway enthusiasts, photographic archives, recollections of ex-Pullman staff and from a wealth of railway literature. All the carriages are different; each has a distinctive personality and has had a varied and eventful life.

Many of the Pullmans in the Venice Simplon-Orient-Express have been used by the royal family. Although there is a special royal train for long journeys, Pullmans were often called into service for shorter journeys, particularly in the south of England. Queen Elizabeth and other members of the royal family often travelled on the Golden Arrow, the Brighton Belle, the Queen of Scots and other famous Pullman services. Sometimes special Pullman trains would be assembled for royal or state occasions. Several of the Pullmans which are now in the Venice Simplon-Orient-Express were used to bring foreign dignitaries to London for the Coronation in 1953, and others have been involved in a variety of national events, including the state visits of French Presidents Auriol in 1950 and de Gaulle in 1960, the visit of the Russian leaders Bulganin and Krushchev in 1956 and the funeral of Sir Winston Churchill in 1965.

Audrey

With her bright chrome fittings, her strip ceiling lights and her twelve different marquetry panels of landscape scenes, *Audrey* is quite unlike any other Pullman in the Venice Simplon-Orient-Express. She was built in 1932 in Birmingham, as a first-class kitchen car. She was made specially for the Southern Belle service between London and Brighton and went into operation on 1 January 1933 as part of the world's first all-electric Pullman train. The Southern Belle, renamed the Brighton Belle a year later, was the oldest all-Pullman service in Europe, dating from 1881. On 9 October 1940 *Audrey* was bomb-damaged during an air-raid on Victoria Station and during her restoration for the Venice

The coat of arms of the Pullman Car Company, formerly painted on every Pullman car, and now restored to the sides of the VS-O-E Pullmans.

Simplon-Orient-Express pieces of shrapnel and glass were found embedded in her marquetry. After the war she was repaired at Birmingham and rejoined the Brighton Belle in 1947. Between 1951 and 1964 she was used regularly by members of the royal family. In 1953 the Queen Mother, Queen Elizabeth and the Duke of Edinburgh travelled in her to Portsmouth for the Coronation Review of the Fleet at Spithead, while in 1964 Queen Elizabeth went on her to Brighton for a royal visit to the new Sussex University.

The state funeral of Sir Winston Churchill took place on 30 January 1965. A special Pullman train, which included Cygnus *and* Perseus, *carried the coffin from Waterloo Station to Long Hanborough in Oxfordshire for the burial service at Bladon.*

[36]

Two of the marquetry landscape panels from Audrey, *built in 1932 for the Brighton Belle.*

Audrey remained in the Brighton Belle service until 30 April 1972, when the Brighton Belle was withdrawn, despite vociferous public outcry spearheaded by such distinguished travellers as Sir Laurence Olivier, who since 1961 had travelled on her regularly between Brighton and the London theatre. The day before the service was closed, a dinner was given in *Audrey* for mourning railway enthusiasts – by all accounts they had a splendid wake. During her service *Audrey* had travelled 2.7 million miles. After being withdrawn she was bought privately from British Rail by David Lowther, a master at Eton College who was determined that at least one of the Brighton Belle carriages should survive in good condition. In 1980 *Audrey* was included in the cavalcade to celebrate the 150th anniversary of the opening of the Liverpool and Manchester Railway. In the same year she was bought by VS-O-E Ltd. When she arrived in Carnforth several of her windows had been smashed. One of the great problems with these beautiful old coaches has been that they are magnets for vandals.

Cygnus

Cygnus, *Carina* and *Perseus* were designed in 1938 but were not actually completed until 1951 for the new Golden Arrow, which was refurbished as part of the Festival of Britain. *Cygnus* was built using 1930s designs and materials put into store before the war. The decoration of rich dark mahogany panels with the grain skilfully matched was by Waring & Gillow. *Cygnus* ran in the Golden Arrow from London to Dover and was included in the Arrow's last run on 30 October 1972. It was also used for royal trains and by heads of state on official visits and was part of Sir Winston Churchill's funeral train in

The lavatory floor of Cygnus, *showing one of the series of mosaics created for the Pullman cars by Marjorie Knowles.*

1965. After being withdrawn it was stored at Brighton while being considered for static restaurant use. *Phoenix* and *Carina* were shipped to France to become roadside diners, but *Cygnus* left storage in Brighton for the Scottish and Newcastle Breweries, Tyneside, in 1973. By 1976 it was in service on the North Yorkshire Moors Railway, a private steam railway. In the same year, together with *Perseus* and *Zena*, it starred in the film *Agatha* (with Vanessa Redgrave and Dustin Hoffman) and appeared in scenes shot in York and Harrogate stations hauled by the famous steam locomotive *Flying Scotsman*, owned by Bill McAlpine. It was given the name *Anne* in the film. In 1977 it was bought by VS-O-E Ltd.

Ibis

Built in 1925, *Ibis* is the oldest carriage in either the British or continental rake. It has become some passengers' favourite with its marquetry medallions of Greek dancing girls and pale blue upholstery. The original marquetry designs were rediscovered by Bob Dunn (the VS-O-E marquetry restorer) among his father's records. As soon as it was completed in October 1925 *Ibis* was sold to the Wagons-Lits Company and shipped across the Channel for service in Italy. Its name was replaced by the number 52 (Pullmans have never had names on the Continent). For two years it operated from Milan to Venice on the Simplon-Orient-Express, and to Nice, and it was transferred to the Deauville Express in 1927. This express had started in 1923 to entice wealthy Parisians to the Deauville Casino and the cars were decked in the famous blue livery that had inspired Sergei Diaghilev to commission the ballet *Le Train Bleu*. The train included four sleeping cars for use in the afternoon run, which caused scandalised comment in the contemporary press. The next summer *Ibis* finished its continental service by running in the Pullman Express between Paris and Ostend. Transferred back to England, it was rebuilt for the Golden Arrow and its name was restored. It was in the Golden Arrow from 1930 until 1952 apart from the war years when it was probably used as a stationary restaurant car by the Royal Navy. From 1952 to 1963 it was part of the Ocean Liner special boat train to Southampton, meeting the *Queen Mary*, *Queen Elizabeth I* or the *United States*. By 1968 it was preserved by the Dart Valley Railway. It was transferred to the Standard Gauge Steam Trust at Tyseley, near Birmingham, in 1970. It was bought for restoration by VS-O-E Ltd from Birmingham Railway Museum in 1981.

King George VI, Queen Elizabeth and Princess Elizabeth and Margaret bid farewell to Queen Mary on their departure for South Africa. The royal party travelled to Portsmouth on 1 February 1947 in Pullman Rosemary. Ibis *was also part of the train.*

Ibis, *the oldest of the VS-O-E Pullmans, built in 1925, is decorated with marquetry medallions of Greek dancing girls.*

Ione

Built in 1928, *Ione* is a very pretty carriage with burr wood panels of ash surmounted by a frieze of Victorian pink roses. She was intended for the Queen of Scots Pullman but by 1929 was running on the Great Western Railway, on the Ocean Liner service to Plymouth and on the Torbay Pullman. From 1931 she was in the Bournemouth Belle and was included in the Southampton boat train, meeting transatlantic liners. From 1948 until the 1960s she worked with the Queen of Scots, the Yorkshire Pullman, the Tees-Tyne Pullman and the South of Wales Pullman. The Queen of Scots, which ran from London's Kings Cross station to Glasgow and Edinburgh, was a particularly prestigious

Ione is decorated with a marquetry frieze of flowers and burr wood panels of ash.

Minerva

Minerva was built in 1927 with distinctively delicate and fragile Edwardian marquetry. She immediately went into service with the Southern Railway and ran on a number of Pullman routes until 1939. She was put into storage during the war and in 1947 joined the new Devon Belle Pullman which ran for the first time on 16 June, linking London with the West Country holiday centres. In 1951 *Minerva* was extensively refurbished to join new carriages built for the Golden Arrow to celebrate the Festival of Britain. She became a first-class parlour car with a guard's compartment, and her windows were redesigned to harmonise with the newer cars. During the early 1950s she was included in special trains for state visits and for royal use and was in frequent service during 1953, bringing visitors from Dover Marine to Victoria for the Coronation of Queen Elizabeth II and later to the Coronation Derby. She was withdrawn from the Golden Arrow in 1961 and preserved privately by the Lytham Creek Railway Museum, Lancashire.

train, frequently used by royalty for their journeys to Scotland for holidays. In 1964 *Ione* joined another crack Pullman, the Talisman, covering 880 miles per day. She was withdrawn from service in 1968 and eventually put up for auction and sold privately for £850 in 1969. She was preserved by P. W. Whitehouse and used for private charter work, based at the Standard Gauge Steam Trust, Tyseley, near Birmingham. In 1981 she was bought for restoration by VS-O-E Ltd from the Birmingham Railway Museum and joined the English Pullmans in December 1982.

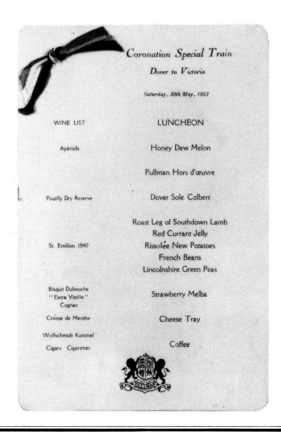

Marquetry reflections in Minerva.

LEFT *Luncheon served on Saturday 30 May 1953 on the Coronation special bringing royal visitors to London.* Minerva *and* Phoenix *ran in this train.*

Perseus

Like *Cygnus*, *Perseus* was designed during the 1930s but was not actually completed until 1951, when it joined the new Golden Arrow as part of the Festival of Britain celebrations. The decor is of elegant yellow wood panels with the grain very skilfully matched. Several old prints of Dover, the White Cliffs and the Shakespeare Tunnel are reminders of the Golden Arrow route. *Perseus* remained in continuous Golden Arrow service and was included in the last run on 30 October 1972. It also joined a number of special trains. On 18 April 1956 it carried the Russian leaders Bulganin and Krushchev back to Portsmouth at the end of their ten-day state visit to Britain, and in 1965 formed part of Sir Winston Churchill's funeral train. By 1976 *Perseus* was preserved on the North Yorkshire Moors Railway, a private steam railway, and in the same year starred in the film *Agatha* together with *Cygnus* and *Zena*. In 1977 it was bought for restoration by VS-O-E Ltd.

The Russian leaders Bulganin and Krushchev left London on a special Pullman train on 27 April 1956 at the end of their state visit. Marshal Bulganin (sitting), accompanied by the British Foreign Secretary Mr Selwyn Lloyd, settles into Pullman Perseus *at Victoria.*

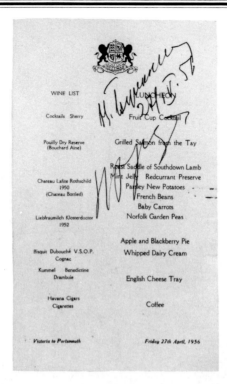

On the journey to Portsmouth Bulganin and Krushchev signed a copy
of the menu for the train's conductor, Albert Jones.

Light fitting and brass luggage racks in Perseus.

Phoenix (ex Rainbow)
In August 1936 a carriage called *Rainbow* was accidentally destroyed by fire at Micheldever in the south of England. The chassis was retained and remained in store until 1952, when it was rebuilt for service with the Golden Arrow, and appropriately renamed *Phoenix*. The decor was originally designed by Mary Adshead but now comprises beautiful marquetry flowers in an oval frame from a design in the Waring & Gillow records found in the Dunns' papers. *Phoenix* remained in Golden Arrow service until 1972, and was included in the last run of the train on 30 October. It was the first choice as royal

Phoenix *was rebuilt in 1952 on the chassis of* Rainbow *(1927).*
The new marquetry panels were made for the V S-O-E *by Bob Dunn,*
the marquetry restorer, from a 1920s design by Waring & Gillow
discovered amongst his father's records.

Queen Elizabeth greets the French President Charles de Gaulle at Victoria Station on 5 April 1960 at the start of his state visit. He travelled in Phoenix.

carriage, and was used on many occasions by the Queen Mother. It was part of the Coronation Special bringing foreign dignitaries to London and later that week took them to the Coronation Derby. In April 1960 General de Gaulle travelled in it on his state visit to Britain. In 1973 *Phoenix* was sold to Hotels-Restaurant Mercure and used as a static restaurant near Lyon in France. It was bought by VS-O-E Ltd in 1980 and transported back to England by road on a giant trailer; in transit it got stuck under a bridge. It had a picture of de Gaulle inside the car and a huge photograph of the Coronation in one of the coupé compartments.

Zena

The marquetry in *Zena* is the most strikingly Art Deco of all the British carriages. In 1929 she was in service with the Great Western Railway on Ocean Liner services to Plymouth and in the Torbay Pullman. Two years later she was with the Southern Railway and continued for some years on Southampton boat trains and with the Bournemouth Belle. After the war, she joined the Queen of Scots, the Yorkshire Pullman and the Tees-Tyne Pullman in 1946. During the 1950s she also worked in the South Wales Pullman. In March 1950 she carried President and Madame Vincent Auriol of France on their state visit to Britain. On their return journey they had 'Filets of Sole Zena' for lunch and President Auriol drafted a letter of thanks to King George VI on the back of the menu card. In 1960 *Zena* joined the Queen of Scots, a train frequently used by royalty on their visits to Scotland, and in August 1965 she was part of the final run of the Tees-Tyne Pullman. The following year *Zena* was saved from the scrap-heap by Terry Robinson of Doncaster. He saw her in the sidings outside York railway works with a white cross painted on her, indicating she had been taken out of service. He knew that after withdrawal coaches were generally sold to scrap merchants. They would remove one of the axle lubricating pads, place it in a downwind toilet compartment and light it, usually on a Friday night. The fire would burn all week-end and nothing would be left except metal to cut up. Terry Robinson felt *Zena* was such a beautiful car that he bought her from British Rail. Eventually he sold her to VS-O-E Ltd for restoration as part of the British train.

Baggage Car No. 7

The car was built by the North Eastern Railway Company in York in 1943 as a van for transporting racing or homing pigeons. It was constructed with a sloping floor so that it could be hosed down easily. Later it became Gresley Brake Van No. E.70741 and was in regular service on the East Coast mainline. In 1954 it was used as the brake van for the Aberdonian and Flying Scotsman trains. Bill McAlpine bought it in 1978 and it was transferred to VS-O-E Ltd in 1980. It was extensively renovated and restored as a teak covered van, but unfortunately the regulations would not permit the car to be surfaced in wood – so the teak had to be covered in turn with metal.

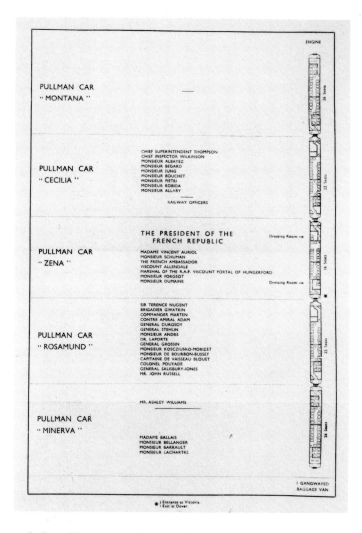

Pullman Zena *was used on a number of royal and state occasions. In March 1950 she was included with* Minerva *in the train that carried French President Vincent Auriol to and from London for his state visit. The seating plan shows that President Auriol travelled in* Zena *from Victoria to Dover Marine.*

VS-O-E Ltd has several more Pullmans at Carnforth which have not yet been restored. Some were beyond repair and have been used as woodworking shops or for spare parts. Others, like *Agatha* (1928), *Carina* (1951), Pullman 154 (1923, rebuilt 1938) and Pullman 286 (1932, ex-Brighton Belle) may be brought back to use in the future.

The refurbished interior of Zena, *built in 1928.*

The passengers catch their first glimpse of the continental train at Boulogne as it waits by the ferry. It is a tremendously long train (1,400 feet, 400 metres) composed of seventeen navy and gold carriages in the traditional livery of the Wagons-Lits Company which was introduced in the late 1920s. The train when operated at its full length is made up of eleven sleeping cars, three restaurant cars (one of them a Pullman), a bar car and two cars used for the staff and baggage. The raised brass lettering on the sides reads 'Compagnie Internationale des Wagons-Lits et des Grands Express Européens', a title first seen on the carriages on the original run of the Orient-Express in 1883. Each car has the Wagons-Lits crest with two lions holding a medallion with 'W' and 'L' entwined. The lions are Belgian, a legacy of Nagelmackers' most important patron, King Leopold II, who gave him permission to use them. Unlike the Pullmans the continental cars have no names, only numbers, and descriptions of their function like 'Voiture-Restaurant'. The descriptions appear in English, French, German and Italian. The total weight of the raised brass lettering on the train is a staggering two tons.

The search for the histories of the continental cars started in the Wagons-Lits archives in Paris. The movements of every individual car had been recorded in a log book, so that it was possible to trace each car in six-month stages throughout its existence, from its manufacture until 1949. After that Wagons-Lits changed its recording system and it was no longer possible to follow the routing of an individual coach in the log books. George Behrend, author of many splendid books on trains and the most enthusiastic of railway historians, has been a great help in tracing the details after 1949.

While it is comparatively easy to identify the English Pullmans, it is much harder to connect Wagons-Lits carriages with particular historical events, because it is much more difficult to remember a number than a name.

In February 1929 the Simplon-Orient-Express was stuck in a snow drift for ten days in Western Turkey. Car 3309 was in service with the Simplon-Orient-Express on this part of the route.

Sleeping Car 3309

The oldest of the sleeping cars is 3309, built in 1926 in Belgium. This originally had eight single and four double compartments, each with lovely marquetry panels by René Prou. It operated exclusively in the Orient-Express, working on various parts of the route from 1928 to 1939, from Paris to Bucharest or Munich, or all the way to Istanbul via Vienna and Budapest. It can be connected to a number of dramatic events during this period.

On 1 February 1929 the Orient-Express was marooned in a snow drift sixty miles from Istanbul for ten days before the snow ploughs got through. It was savagely cold and communications broke down all over Europe. I have an account of the passengers' ordeal from Mrs Beth Vinding, who was travelling on the train from Copenhagen to Istanbul with her family. Her husband was a civil engineer, helping to build new railways in Anatolia as part of Ataturk's radical industrialisation policy for Turkey. Their journey took fourteen days instead of the four scheduled in the timetable.

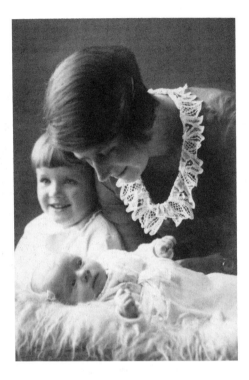

Mrs Beth Vinding was marooned with her husband and two children on the snow-bound Orient-Express. This photograph was taken just before they set off for Istanbul.

'I had returned to Denmark to have my second child late in 1928 as notions of hygiene in Turkey were very rudimentary. My husband joined me for Christmas and we all left Copenhagen for Stambul in late January. At Berlin we took a two-berth compartment in the sleeper. I slept in the top bunk with Jørgen, my four-year-old, while the new baby was in a hammock between the luggage racks and my husband took the lower bunk. At Belgrade our sleeping car was joined to the train from France, which included a beautiful dining car. It had been snowing hard throughout the journey but in the Balkans it became worse and by the third day, when we were travelling through the high mountains of the European part of Turkey, the situation looked grim. The train stopped at a station called Alpullu and, although the snow was not too deep, we were told that we had to stay there overnight. The temperature was − 20 degrees centigrade.

Next morning we awoke to a blue sky and bright sunshine but the train still did not move. The line was blocked by deep snow a few kilometres ahead and by another Orient-Express buried somewhere in that snow. We stayed at Alpullu for nine days and during the first week other trains came in behind us every day so that finally, before they stopped coming, there were nine trains in one long row, stretching back from the station. Luckily Alpullu was a good place to stop because there was a sugar mill by the station which had a restaurant willing to serve the trapped passengers one hot meal a day. But for that we might have starved. One meal a day, however, is not enough for a growing four-year-old, but thank God that my mother, pessimistic about the dreadful weather, had packed some Quaker Oats for us at the last minute. Thanks to her I could give Jørgen porridge every morning and I managed to feed another child on the train as well.

Naturally the dining car had not anticipated feeding us for such a long time, and quickly ran out of food. The unshaven waiters could only give us tea and that was not before eleven in the morning. We could buy bread from Turkish peasants who walked from their villages, eager to do some business with the passengers of the famous train, and we ate this in the dining car with our ration of tea.

Everybody was very kind to us because we had young children. When the heating pipes in our compartment froze solid we were allowed to move to a warm one, and an elderly gentleman amused Jørgen for hours by putting the last part of every cigarette he smoked into the funnel of a toy steam engine he had been given for Christmas.

Water was a serious problem, but my husband found a steam outlet somewhere on the locomotive whose boiler was kept stoked and by holding a bottle over this he collected enough hot water to melt a lump of snow in our basin, allowing me to wash the baby's clothes. The drying was done on a piece of string between two freight cars.

After nine days at Alpullu we were told that the train would leave for Stambul in half an hour, as a snow plough had been sent to our rescue. We took down our makeshift washing-line, and the train left the station. But the snow became deeper and deeper until eventually we ground to a halt at Chataldya. We were marooned in the snow, buried in mountainous drifts higher than the train itself.

The conductor told us that the snow plough had been derailed and we became really very worried. It looked as though we were going to have to sit it out until the snow melted with no friendly sugar mill to sell us food. Fortunately our fears were groundless as the snow plough was put back on the rails and slowly, very slowly, we crawled safely into Stambul. For the first time in a fortnight we washed, had a good meal and slept in a hotel room which, after the cramped train compartment, seemed truly gigantic. It was certainly a journey I shall never forget.'

Sleeping Car 3309 may also have been involved in a very serious incident in 1931. The carriage was running all the way from Bucharest to Boulogne and was possibly part of the Orient-Express that left Budapest for Paris on the evening of 12 September. Shortly after leaving the Hungarian capital the train was crossing the viaduct of Biatorbagy when a bomb exploded, plunging the engine and nine carriages into a deep ravine. A coupling broke and five carriages remained miraculously on the bridge. Over twenty people were killed instantly and over 120 were badly injured. Among the survivors was the cabaret dancer Josephine Baker who attempted to calm the trapped passengers by singing to them. The fascist Hungarian government immediately announced that the bomb had been planted by communists and that they had found an incriminating note on the track near the catastrophe. There was a series of arrests, but some time later a curious silence fell upon the official spokesman. Eventually it was reported that a former Hungarian army officer, avidly pro-fascist, called Sylvester Matsuka, had been arrested for attempting another train bombing in Austria. He boasted about the bombing at Biatorbagy and claimed that the Holy Spirit and three Archangels had ordered his mission. He was trying to derail trains 'to punish atheists travelling on luxury trains and to free the world from Communism'. This somewhat contradictory statement led to doubts about his sanity but he was eventually hanged in 1936.

At the outbreak of war sleeping car 3309 was in Paris and later it was repaired at the Wagons-Lits works at St Denis on the outskirts of Paris. It was in Germany from 1942 to 1945, and then reported '*à rechercher*' in the Wagons-Lits log book – 'Lost, being looked for'. It appeared again as part of the Orient-Express in 1946, having presumably been repatriated from Germany, and stayed with the train, going from Paris to Prague or Gdynia until it was transferred to Portugal in 1958 and based in Lisbon. At Irun (the Spanish Wagons-Lits workshops) the single cabins were modified to give a total of twenty-four berths and the carriage became part of the Sud Express from Irun to Lisbon. Finally it was withdrawn from service in 1971.

Built in 1926, sleeping car 3309 is the oldest of the VS-O-E sleeping cars. The marquetry designed by René Prou, a master of the Art Deco period, is outstanding.

On 12 September 1931 the westbound Orient-Express was derailed while crossing a viaduct near Budapest which had been sabotaged by a Hungarian fascist. The locomotive and nine cars were hurled into the ravine, leaving five cars still on the viaduct. Car 3309 was in the Orient-Express on this part of the route.

Sleeping Car 3425

The second sleeping car in the Venice Simplon-Orient-Express with some single cabins (S-type) ran on many more routes than 3309, switching from service to service all over Europe. It was built in England in 1929 and shipped to the Continent for service there. From 1930 until 1940 it was in the Rome Express, the Orient-Express (from Boulogne to Karlovy-Varna and from Paris to Istanbul), the Arlberg-Orient-Express, and the Engadine-Oberland-Express from Paris to Chur (taking skiers to Davos and St Moritz) and finished up in the Simplon-Orient-Express, running from Istanbul through to Italy (the S-O-E continued to run even after the outbreak of war, as Italy was still technically neutral at that time).

During this twilight period in Europe, with just a few luxury services still running, King Carol of Romania's life-long involvement with the Orient-Express reached its climax when, in the autumn of 1940, he escaped from Bucharest with three railway carriages loaded with booty attached to the Simplon-Orient-Express. Carol's father, King Ferdinand I, was a railway enthusiast who often took his son on the Orient-Express to England or to the Riviera. Carol was a dashing figure, well known for his love affairs, and used the Orient-Express whenever he needed to escape the strictures of court life, or to pack off a discarded lover. His first marriage to a commoner, Zizi Lambrino, was annulled by his father and, even though the unfortunate girl was pregnant, she was dispatched to Paris on the Orient-Express. Carol then became involved with Magda Lupescu, who was to influence the rest of his life. She was married to a Romanian army officer at that time. It was rumoured that she was a descendant of Carol's grandfather by an illicit liaison, and this added spice to the gossip as Carol and Magda may have been first cousins. King Ferdinand stepped in again and arranged for Carol to marry the beautiful Princess Helen of Greece, whom he went to meet on the Orient-Express. Despite the fact that they had a son, Michael, Carol continued to meet Magda, and by 1925 the affair had created so much scandal that he renounced his right to the throne, abandoned his family and took the Orient-Express to Paris to live there with his mistress. Carol divorced Helen in 1928 but by that time Ferdinand was dead and Carol's six-year-old son Michael had been named king, with his mother as regent. Carol was torn between the bewitching Magda Lupescu and the throne he had renounced. Two years later he returned to Romania (for once by air) and seized the throne. There were rumours of a reconciliation between

King Carol of Romania, a great train enthusiast, was a frequent traveller on the Orient-Express. He is shown leaving the station on a state visit to Poland (wearing a cockade), followed by Crown Prince Michael. In 1940 he escaped from Romania with his mistress, Magda Lupescu, on the Orient-Express in which sleeping car 3425 was running.

him and Helen but, although the Romanian government had specifically barred Magda from the country, she returned unheralded on the Orient-Express a month later, to be installed by Carol in a magnificent villa linked to the palace by a tunnel. After this the divorced queen and the uncrowned mistress polarised the political axis of the disturbed country. In 1933 Helen, who had become the figurehead of the anti-king faction, was forced by Carol to leave Bucharest. She was surreptitiously escorted to the darkened station, where she was put on board the Orient-Express for exile in Florence.

Carol retained the throne until 1940 when Romania was divided by Hitler and Stalin and he was forced to abdicate. He left the country with Magda Lupescu on the night of 8 September 1940. Two saloons and a sleeping car were stuffed with treasures from the royal palace, including valuable paintings, stamp collections, books, jewellery and Magda's suitcase full of foreign currency. Partisans shot at the train in

Yugoslavia, but it came through northern Italy unharmed to reach the safety of neutral Switzerland through the Simplon Tunnel.

By the end of 1940 the Simplon-Orient-Express stopped running and sleeping car 3425 was transferred to the Wagons-Lits department at Istanbul. It ran in Turkey (Asia Minor) from Haydarpassa to Ankara in the Anatolian Express and from 1949 until the late 1950s it was in the Aegean Express from Ankara to Ismir and the Taurus Express from Ankara to Adana. Eventually, like so many of the other continental cars, it was transferred to Portugal, where it was modernised and became part of the Sud Express. It ended its life as a 'runner' in reserve at Lisbon.

Detail of the marquetry decoration in the British-built sleeping car 3425, dating from 1929.

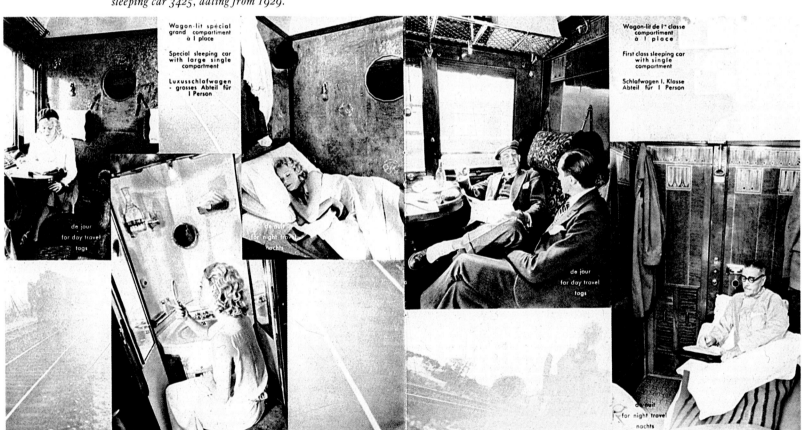

A Wagons-Lits advertising brochure of 1931 shows a car with single cabins with the same marquetry as 3425 [right]. On the left is a Luxe-type sleeping with René Prou decor which is the same as sleeping cars 3525, 3539, 3543 and 3544 in the VS-O-E.

Detail of the 'flower garland' marquetry designed by Morison in the British-built car 3473, built in 1929.

Sleeping Car 3473

In 1929 a new design of sleeping car was ordered by Lord Dalziel, in the famous Lx or Luxe series, to replace the old wooden-bodied carriages running in the Train Bleu and the Simplon-Orient-Express. The carriages were originally designed with ten compartments (Lx 10), each with a single berth, but generally they were converted later to sleep sixteen or twenty by adding an extra bunk. They had the largest sleeping compartments ever built for the European railway system. Only ninety cars were built to this Lx specification, some in England and some in France. All the remaining sleeping cars in the Venice Simplon-Orient-Express come from this renowned series.

Sleeping car 3473 was built in Birmingham in 1929. The marquetry interior was designed by Morison and has charming garlands of flowers zig-zagging as a frieze around the cabins and along the corridor. It started service in the Train Bleu, the famous luxury train linking Paris with the Riviera. The service had been launched in 1922 by René Nagelmackers and had boosted the profits of the Casino in Monte Carlo, as all the smart set flocked to the Côte d'Azur on the glamorous train. Car 3473 linked passengers from the Golden Arrow by taking them from Calais to Paris and then on to the Mediterranean by next morning. In 1937 it joined the Nord Express for two years, running from Paris via Berlin to Niegoreloye on the Russian border. During the war it was stored in France at Lourdes and in 1946 it returned to the Train Bleu until 1961. It finished its service in the Simplon-Orient-Express, being withdrawn in 1971.

CIE DU NORD . WAGONS-LITS . CIE P.L.M.

LE NOUVEAU TRAIN BLEU VERS LA COTE D'AZUR

Poster by Zenobel (1928) for the Train Bleu from Calais to the Côte d'Azur.
Cars 3473, 3482, 3483, 3525, 3539, 3543 and 3544 ran on this route.

*Detail of the 'trapeze' marquetry in the British-built car 3482,
dating from 1929, decorated by Maple, with an Art Deco luggage rack.*

*Detail of the 'flower basket' marquetry designed by Morison,
in the British-built car 3483, dating from 1929.*

Sleeping Car 3482

It was built in England in 1929 with decor by Maple in an abstract
geometrical design called 'Trapeze'. It is almost certain that the
marquetry was executed by Albert Dunn (the father of the marquetry
restorer for the VS-O-E) as his account book shows a bill to Maple in
1928 for 'mauve veneer and green strappings' and Bob Dunn found
identical veneers in his father's stock when he renovated some panels
from 3482.

The car went immediately into the Train Bleu and later alternated
between that and the Rome Express, generally being based at Calais.
In 1937 it was transferred to the Nord Express from Paris to Riga.
This was a rigorous route in winter because the salt from the track
attacked the metalwork on the coaches causing severe corrosion which
showed up at the time of restoration. Cars 3473 and 3483, which also
ran on the Nord route, were also found to be badly corroded. During
the war car 3482 was used as a hotel at Lyon. After the war it was
refurbished at St Denis, the Wagons-Lits workshop on the borders of
Paris, and rejoined the Train Bleu until 1961. Then it did some runs in
the Lombardy Express from Paris to Venice and joined the Simplon-
Orient-Express until 1969. At that point, like so many cars now
running in the VS-O-E, it transferred to the Iberian Peninsula to the
Costa Vasca Express from Madrid to Santander until 1971.

Sleeping Car 3483

This car was built in Birmingham in 1929 and decorated by Morison
with a delightful pattern of flowers clustered in a variety of baskets.
The colours of the veneers are very similar to 3473 and 3482 and it
seems very likely that all three designs were executed by Albert Dunn
in 1928 when he was making marquetry for both Maple and Morison.
During the 1930s the car was in the Train Bleu, the Rome Express and
the Nord Express. At the beginning of the war it was stored at
Pouancée but by 1942 it was rented to Germany. In 1945 the archives
reported '*à rechercher*' – Wagons-Lits had lost track of it, like many
other carriages at that troubled time – but it was eventually recovered
from the German Army in 1946. In the start-up of luxury services
again after the war it went from Paris to Rome, Biarritz and Brig and
from 1948 it was in the Simplon-Orient-Express. It ran in the Costa
Brava Express from 1973 to 1977.

A poster for a musical comedy reflecting the popular idea of what went on in the train.

One of the inlaid Art Deco motifs, known as 'Sapelli Pearl', in the Luxe sleeping cars decorated by René Prou. The inlay was plaster of Paris.

Sleeping Car 3525

The next four carriages were all built in France and decorated in a similar pattern by René Prou, a leading designer of the Art Deco period. Each compartment has elegant circles of stylised flowers in an ivory-like inlay set in a chequer-board design. The inlay is neither wood nor ivory but was made from plaster of Paris which has aged and slightly cracked over the years. The technique is known as parquetry.

Born in Nantes in 1889, Prou later taught in Paris, where he developed an individual style for interiors and furniture which was decorative without too much ornamentation. His style was well suited to the sophisticated French scene of the 1920s, with its combination of traditional craftsmanship, modern techniques and exotic materials. He exhibited in the Paris Exhibition of 1925 which launched the Art Deco movement and by the 1930s he had an international reputation. He was commissioned to decorate the interior of Mitsubishi department store in Tokyo, the dining room in the Waldorf Astoria, New York, and the council chamber for the League of Nations in Geneva. He also designed interiors for liners as well as Wagons-Lits sleepers.

Car 3525 went briefly into service on the Pyrénées Côte d'Argent Express which ran from Paris to the fashionable resort of Biarritz. The Duke of Windsor enhanced its popularity between the wars because he preferred Biarritz to the Côte d'Azur. From 1930 to 1939 the car alternated between the Train Bleu and the Rome Express and was stored through the war at Lourdes. It returned to the Train Bleu from 1946 to 1948 and from 1961 to 1969. In between it was in the Simplon-Orient-Express and the Rome Express. It was transferred to Spain in 1969 and stayed with the Costa Vasca Express until it was withdrawn in 1972.

Sleeping Car 3539

This car has the same decoration by René Prou as car 3525. It was in the Pyrénées Côte d'Argent Express for one year and then transferred to the Train Bleu in 1930. In 1932 it was converted from a Lx 10 to a Lx 16 by the addition of six berths, but the Depression was biting into luxury travel and Wagons-Lits found they had surplus cars. Car 3539 was withdrawn and stored until 1936, when it joined the Rome Express. It was stored in Paris during the war and used by the US Army Transportation Corps between 1945 and 1947. It ran in the Mozart Express in 1947. Later in 1947 it joined the Simplon-Orient-Express and Rome Express until 1971, when it was withdrawn.

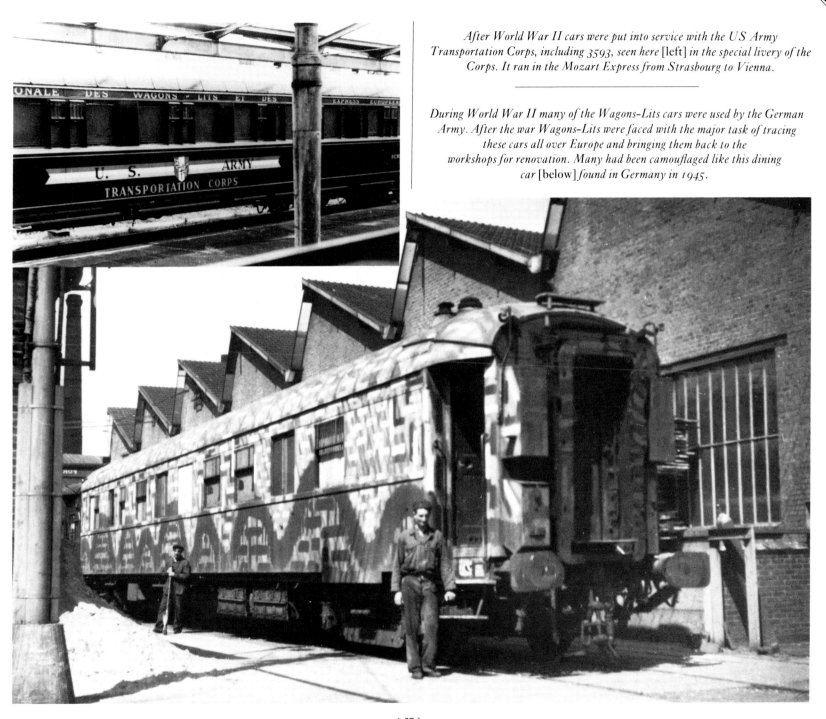

After World War II cars were put into service with the US Army Transportation Corps, including 3593, seen here [left] in the special livery of the Corps. It ran in the Mozart Express from Strasbourg to Vienna.

During World War II many of the Wagons-Lits cars were used by the German Army. After the war Wagons-Lits were faced with the major task of tracing these cars all over Europe and bringing them back to the workshops for renovation. Many had been camouflaged like this dining car [below] found in Germany in 1945.

A sleeping compartment in car 3543 in its night-time configuration, showing a number of the René Prou inlaid motifs.

Sleeping car 3544 has an extra large lavatory. This car was used as a brothel in Limoges during the war and was in the Dutch royal train from 1946 to 1948.

Sleeping Car 3543

This car was built in France, decorated by René Prou, and went into service on the Pyrénées Côte d'Argent Express and the Train Bleu until 1932. It was withdrawn during the Depression, returning to service on the Rome Express. After the war it rejoined the Train Bleu from 1950 to 1956 and finished service in the Simplon-Orient-Express from 1961 to 1969. It was bought for VS-O-E Ltd by James Sherwood at the Monte Carlo auction in 1977 and was one of the first two sleeping cars to form the nucleus of rolling stock for the VS-O-E.

Sleeping Car 3544

Another carriage in the group decorated by René Prou, car 3544 had a varied and dramatic existence. It went first into the Pyrénées-Côte d'Argent Express and the Train Bleu, taking the rich and glamorous to the French coasts. It was stored during the Depression at St Denis, Paris, and emerged to enter service between Paris and Marseilles with the Rome Express. During the war the car was stored at Limoges where it was used as a brothel, let out by an enterprising local official. In 1946 it was elevated to become part of the royal Dutch train – a

One of the oval marquetry panels, designed by Nelson,
in the corridors of cars 3552, 3553 and 3555.

Poster showing the connections possible via the Simplon-Orient-Express. Thirteen
VS-O-E cars were in the S-O-E at some time in their history, including 3552.

change of scene indeed. Queen Wilhelmina had been given her first royal train as a wedding present in 1901, and had used it extensively for forty years. When the Germans invaded the Low Countries in 1940 her train was requisitioned. When it was returned it had been looted and was in such a terrible condition that it could not be used again as a royal train. Car 3544 was sent up to Amsterdam from Paris to join the new Dutch royal train, where it remained from the summer of 1946 until 12 March 1948. After this exhilarating period it returned to the Train Bleu for two years and then alternated with the Simplon-Orient-Express from Calais to Trieste. George Behrend reported that he saw it in the Train Bleu at Calais in April 1960.

Sleeping Car 3552

The remaining three sleeping cars were all built in France and decorated by Nelson with a delicate tracery of tiger-lilies and small mauve flower heads. On the outside of the cabin doors in the corridors are oval plaques of more stylised flowers with long stems, some faded by the sunshine. These cars have very pretty chrome luggage racks with the flower motif in relief.

Car 3552 was in the Pyrénées-Côte d'Argent Express for the whole of the 1930s, garaged at Lourdes at the beginning of the war and finished the war as a hotel at Lyon. It ran briefly in the Etoile du Nord in 1945, in boat trains to Brest and in the Simplon-Orient-Express from 1946 to 1949. It had a long run in the Nord Express from 1949 to 1969 and was eventually transferred to Madrid, like many of the other sleeping cars, to complete service in the Costa Vasca Express.

Sleeping Car 3553

Car 3553 had the same history as the previous car, with pre-war service in the Pyrénées-Côte d'Argent Express and then being used as an hotel at Lyons. From 1945 it had four years with the Paris-Brest boat train at the period when Brest was an international port for ocean liners. From 1949 until 1961 it was with the Simplon-Orient-Express. It was finally transferred to Lisbon into the Sud Express from 1969 until 1971 when it was withdrawn.

Sleeping Car 3555

Car 3555 probably ran in the same group as 3552 and 3553 as their histories in the Wagons-Lits archives are almost identical. The only difference is that car 3555 was in the Nord Express from 1961 until

The tiger-lily marquetry in car 3553 designed by Nelson, built in France in 1929.

1969 when, like the others, it was transferred to the Sud Express working out of Lisbon to Irun and Hendaye. It was withdrawn in 1971 and bought for restoration from Wagons-Lits in 1981.

There are four public cars in the Venice Simplon-Orient-Express continental rake, distinguished externally from the sleeping cars by their cream paintwork above the waist of the carriage. (The sleeping cars are all navy up to the cream roofs.)

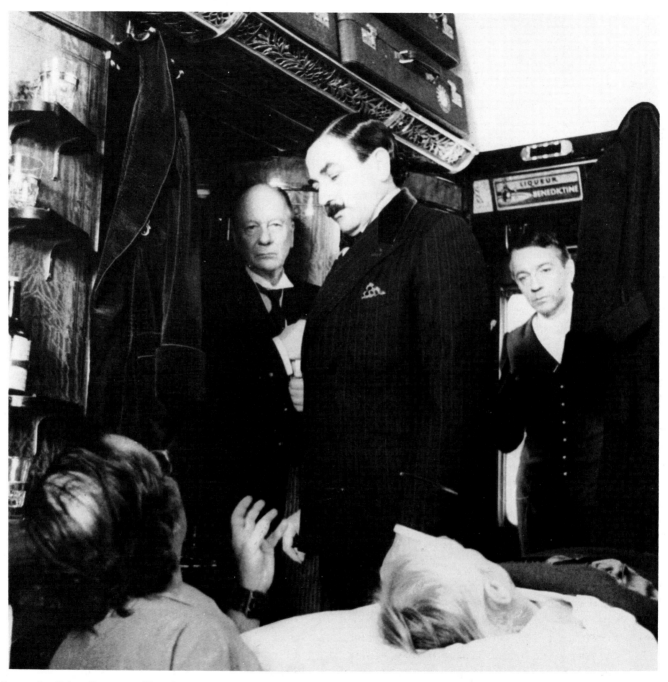

Filming Murder on the Orient Express. *Albert Finney as Hercule Poirot, watched by John Gielgud and Jean-Pierre Cassel, prepares to examine Richard Widmark (the much-stabbed corpse). Sleeping car 3504, shown here, was in the same series as 3552–3555 and has identical luggage racks designed by Nelson.*

Detail of the luggage rack in car 3555, designed by Nelson. The flowers in the casting match the tiger-lily marquetry, and are the same as those in the still from the film Murder on the Orient Express.

Dining Car 4095 – 'Voiture Chinoise'

Wagon-Restaurant 4095 was originally a Pullman kitchen car built in 1927 in Birmingham in the 'Etoile du Nord' style, but with less distinguished marquetry panels than dining car 4110, which was also built there for the Etoile du Nord. Lord Dalziel had ordered both these Pullmans to be built in England just before his death. At that time he was a dominant figure on the boards of both Wagons-Lits and the British Pullman Car Company and he particularly wanted continental Pullmans to be built in England rather than in France.

When car 4095 was bought for the VS-O-E the interior was replaced by black lacquer panels that had been in dining car 3583. The black panels which now line the interior were found in Madrid by James Sherwood, and although they came from a carriage that had been built in France by Entreprises Industrielles Charantaises Aytré, La Rochelle, one year later, they fitted exactly into car 4095.

Dining car 4095 was shipped from the builders to France and entered the Etoile du Nord. This was an all-Pullman service between Paris and Amsterdam, passing through Brussels, a journey of 350 miles. It was a supremely comfortable trip, leaving Paris before noon with a leisurely lunch on the way, relaxing in the capacious chairs for a doze and then arriving in Amsterdam in time for dinner.

Car 4095 was then transferred to the brand new Edelweiss Train de Luxe which started on 15 June 1928, running from Amsterdam to Basle and on to Lucerne. This was another very popular all-Pullman route with good connections from London via Harwich. Car 4095 only stayed in the Edelweiss for the service's first summer and was then transferred back to the Etoile du Nord for the winter of 1928–9. In the summer of 1929 it was used for the inauguration of yet another Train de Luxe, L'Oiseau Bleu, which started on 15 May on the route from Paris via Brussels to Antwerp.

Poster designed by Cassandre in 1927 advertising the Etoile du Nord service. Cars 3552, 3553, 4095, 4110 and 4141 ran on this route.

After L'Oiseau Bleu car 4095 joined another service which only operated for three seasons. This was the London-Vichy Pullman Express. The service was an early victim of the Depression which caused a number of Trains de Luxe routes to be abandoned and by 1930 it was in its last year of operation to Vichy.

Every winter dining car 4095 returned to the Etoile du Nord service and was re-assigned during the summer months to yet another all-Pullman service. In the summer of 1931 it was part of the Oberland Pullman from Paris to Berne and Interlaken. This train carried tourists to the Alpine resorts of Mürren, Grindelwald and Wengen.

During the next winter of 1931–2 the car was based in Brussels and ran in the Calais to Brussels Pullman Express. The train waited at Calais for the arrival of the *Canterbury*, the special ferry built for carrying all-Pullman passengers from the Golden Arrow across the Channel. Some of the passengers would board the Flèche d'Or and others would climb onto the rake of Pullmans going to Brussels.

In the summer of 1932 car 4095 became part of the Flèche d'Or connecting Calais and Paris. The train ran empty from Paris via Boulogne to Calais, where it picked up passengers from the *Canterbury*. This is almost the same route that the Venice Simplon-Orient-Express continental rake runs today.

The Côte d'Azur Pullman Express had been inaugurated in December 1929 and Pullman 4095 joined it for the winter season of 1932–3. It was a very glamorous train which left Paris for Nice and Menton and became identified with the Roaring Twenties rather in the same way as the Train Bleu. Another Venice Simplon-Orient-Express car was already in the rake, Pullman dining car 4141, which had been specially designed for the service by René Lalique. The most famous poster for the Côte d'Azur Pullman was by Pierre Fix-Masseau, who has done the posters for the VS-O-E today. The Côte d'Azur had been made popular particularly by the English. Queen Victoria had kept her royal railway carriage at Calais for years to take her down to Nice and she made the Côte d'Azur a fashionable place to stay in the winter. For the remaining years of the thirties car 4095 was exclusively involved with two Trains de Luxe. In the summer time it

---

One of the black lacquer panels that make car 4095, the 'Voiture Chinoise', so distinctive and so redolent of the 1920s.
(These black lacquer panels came from the wrecked dining car 3583).

was part of the Etoile du Nord, operating out of Brussels, and in the winter it was switched to the Flèche d'Or. This shifting of rolling stock from service to service seems to have been a common practice of Wagons-Lits and it certainly made historical research difficult. The wartime history of car 4095 was very complicated. It was at Cambrée until mid-1942, then at St Denis, l'Ardoise, Eymet and lastly stored at Villeneuve until 1946. It went back into continuous service on the restored Etoile du Nord from the summer of 1946 until 1951.

It was transferred to Portugal in 1951, but had to have its bogies altered at Irun, where there is a Wagons-Lits workshop, before it could run in the Iberian Peninsula. The car joined the Sud Express and was based in Lisbon, working from Lisbon to Medina del Campo in Spain. There it would be uncoupled to return to Lisbon next day as the diner in the westbound Sud Express.

The Sud Express became one of the most important pre-World War I routes. Nagelmackers had announced as early as 1884 his intention to create a 'Nord-Sud' Express to run from St Petersburg to Lisbon. He hoped to avoid the change of trains required at the Spanish border because of the different gauges by developing special equipment (which was not actually introduced until 1969). The Sud-Express started on 4 November 1887, and the Nord-Express not until ten years later on 1 May 1897. The problem of the different gauges was solved by a train from Paris going to Irun, the passengers then changing onto Spanish sleeping cars and the French train returning with passengers travelling northbound from Lisbon. It had the highest occupancy rate of all luxury trains before World War I so that Royal Mail services and the Union Castle Line reorganised their sailings from Lisbon to Rio de Janeiro, Buenos Aires and Dakar to fit in with the train's schedule.

The passenger list was very distinguished. On one day in 1902 the train carried the Imperial Grand Duke Vladimir of Russia, His Highness Albert of Prussia, a delegation from Siam, Prince Christian of Denmark, the Prince of Monaco and Count Moltke. The service was interrupted by World War I and some of the cars were sequestered for Marshal Foch's special train. After the war the train was as popular as ever, with Biarritz gaining in fashion as the Côte d'Argent was patronised by King Edward VII. Because of this increased traffic a Sud Express composed of Pullman cars was started in August 1926 and ran to Biarritz. The Spanish part of the Sud Express was affected by the Civil War in Spain and stopped running for a year from July 1936.

King Boris of Bulgaria was such a dedicated train enthusiast that he often exercised his royal right to drive the Orient-Express as it passed through his kingdom. Dining car 4110 was based in Bucharest during the 1930s and may well have been driven by the royal engine driver. He is shown opening a new railway line in northern Bulgaria. After giving his speech he drove the engine on its first run.

After World War II Madrid became linked to Lisbon by the Lusitania Express, a Train de Luxe which included dining car 4110 from 1961 to 1969.

Wagons-Lits had a substantial organisation in Spain and Portugal and many of the Venice Simplon-Orient-Express sleepers were originally in use there. Sleeping cars 3309, 3425, 3482, 3525, 3552, 3553, 3555 and dining cars 4095 and 4110 were all part of Wagons-Lits' Spanish or Portuguese rolling stock in their later years and many were still runners, albeit in need of complete overhaul and restoration, when bought for the Venice Simplon-Orient-Express.

Dining Car 4110 – 'Etoile du Nord'

Perhaps the most beautiful marquetry in the continental rake is found in the Etoile du Nord dining car 4110. This was built in 1926 in England by Birmingham Railway and Carriage and Wagon Co.,

Smethwick, in the same workshop as Pullman dining car 4095 and *Ibis*. The marquetry was made by Bob Dunn's father in London. The cost of preparing the marquetry for a carriage of this type in 1925 was about £70. Bob Dunn repaired and restored a great deal of the marquetry on the Venice Simplon-Orient-Express and was even able to find matching veneer used by his father in the 1920s. One panel in this car has been completely remade – but it is hard to be sure which one it is.

For some reason car 4110 did not immediately go into service on the Continent but appears in the Wagons-Lits log book as 'available' for 1927 to 1928. By the summer of 1928 it was part of the Etoile du Nord from Paris to Amsterdam and then switched to the Edelweiss, based in Amsterdam for the winter season of 1928–9. It then parted company with dining car 4095 and was sent to Bucharest in Romania as part of the Danube Express or the 'Danubiu Pullman Rapide'. This was an all-Pullman Express from Bucharest to Constanza on the Black Sea and to Galati about 100 miles inland on the Danube. It remained in this service until the spring of 1933 except for one summer in the Carpathian Express. The Carpathian Express was an unsuccessful experiment, leaving Brasov high in the Carpathian Mountains at 5.30 a.m. to arrive at Bucharest at 8.50 a.m. and returning late in the evening. In May 1933 the car was in the inaugural run of the Rapid King Carol I Pullman. This was to become the most popular service in Romania. It ran along the Black Sea from the resorts of Constanza, Mangalia and Carmen Sylva, arriving at 10 a.m. in Bucharest and returning from there in the evening. It was so popular that in the summer months it generally had extra Wagons-Lits dining cars added to it and it was regarded with similar affection to that devoted to the Brighton Belle in England.

Dining car 4110 continued to run in Romania in the early part of the war until it was placed in reserve in Bucharest in 1942. It was not retrieved and returned to Paris until 1949 when Wagons-Lits' contract with the Romanian railways ran out, as the Company had been unable to get it back earlier through the Iron Curtain. It was then sent to Slykens, the Wagons-Lits repair shop at Ostend, where all the Lx sleeping cars have been restored for the VS-O-E. It was remodelled as a thirty-eight-seat diner and sent to Portugal to be based in Lisbon. Its bogies had to be changed to accommodate the Iberian gauge. It became part of the Lusitania Express from Lisbon to Madrid until 1969. In the early 1970s, after further remodelling to make forty-one seats, it finished service in Spain, running between Cadiz and Seville.

Interior view of dining car 4110, built for the Etoile du Nord service.

CIE DES CHEMINS DE FER DE PARIS A LYON ET A LA MEDITERRANEE

CIE INTERNATIONALE DES WAGONS LITS

FIX-MASSEAU 29

CÔTE D'AZUR
PULLMAN – EXPRESS

ARTCURIAL CENTRE D'ART PLASTIQUE CONTEMPORAIN 9 AVENUE MATIGNON PARIS

*Poster designed in 1929 by Pierre Fix-Masseau advertising
the Côte d'Azur Pullman.*

Dining Car 4141 – Lalique Pullman

The remaining dining car in the Venice Simplon-Orient-Express continental rake has been restored with the large Pullman chairs. Dining car 4141 was built in 1929 as a first-class Pullman and was decorated by René Lalique in the 'Côte d'Azur' style. He mounted panels of glass depicting 'Bacchanalian maidens' into the mahogany sides of the car. The faintly blue opaque glass shows various classical figures holding grapes, with a matching frieze of smaller panels. Lalique was also responsible for the design of some of the Pullman chairs and for the 'Tulip' light shades throughout the train.

The car went into the Côte d'Azur Pullman Express immediately, for the winter season of 1929–30, and then switched to the Deauville Express. It returned to the Côte d'Azur Pullman for the next winter season and again in 1934–5. During the summers of 1932 and 1933 it was part of the Paris–Vichy Pullman – a service that was shortly to be withdrawn owing to the Depression. It joined the Sud Express in late 1933, going from Paris to Irun on the Spanish border. From 1935 until the beginning of the war it was constantly on L'Oiseau Bleu, mostly working out of Amsterdam to Paris. It was stored throughout the war at Cambrée, Lourdes, l'Ardoise, Eymet and finally Villeneuve. As soon as the Etoile du Nord was restarted in 1946 it ran on the route from Paris to Amsterdam. The Flèche d'Or had started again in May 1946 and the Pullman joined it in 1947. It ran from Paris to Calais for many years, meeting the passengers from the Golden Arrow as it does today for the Venice Simplon-Orient-Express. By 1961 it was in a reserve pool used for special services and in 1971 it was stored at the Wagons-Lits works at Villeneuve. It was rescued from a cold and dreary siding in 1981 by VS-O-E Ltd and restored at Bremen. The Lalique panels were still there, although the car must have been remodelled as it had a curious coupé arrangement. The panels were carefully removed, re-silvered and stored until the rest of the car had been refurbished and they could be safely replaced. Six weeks before the inaugural trip of the Venice Simplon-Orient-Express in May 1982 half the panels were stolen from a locked shed – so for the first year the Pullman car had only half its complement of lovely translucent Bacchanalian maidens.

RIGHT *Panels designed by René Lalique, showing 'Bacchanalian Maidens',
mounted in Pullman dining car 4141.*

The interior of Bar Car 3647 was created by Gérard Gallet in the Art Nouveau style.

Bar Car 3674

Bar car 3674 started as a dining car built in France in 1931. There is no record of the decor at that time and its present appearance has been created for the Venice Simplon-Orient-Express by Gérard Gallet in the Art Nouveau style.

From 1931 it was based at the Gare Saint Lazare in Paris and used to meet the transatlantic liners docking at Le Havre, Cherbourg and Dieppe. The *Transatlantiques* were trains organised around the arrival times of the Cunard boats at Cherbourg Maritime and the United States Lines and the French Line at Le Havre Docks.

Bar Car 3674 was used in domestic services in France during the German occupation. After the war it ran in the Sud Express from Paris to Irun on the Spanish border and from Paris to Toulouse in La Capitole. It was also used on special pilgrimage trains, taking groups of invalids to seek a cure at Lourdes. It ended up running from Paris (Nord) to Calais Maritime, operating as a snack bar in the Flèche d'Or.

There are still a number of cars on the Continent which have not yet been restored. These include the second sleeping car bought at the Monte Carlo auction (3489) which has the same 'Flower Basket' design as 3483, and a car from the train that Hitler kept ready in France for his triumphal entry into Britain. They may be restored eventually to add to the continental rolling stock.

SUMMARY OF DATA ON THE VS-O-E CARRIAGES

KEY

Where Built

Belgium	Les Ateliers de Construction Métallurgique, Nivelles, Belgium
B'ham UK	Birmingham Railway Carriage and Wagon Co. Ltd, Smethwick, Birmingham, England
France	Entreprises Industrielles Charentaises Aytré, La Rochelle, France
LNER UK	London North Eastern Railway, York, England
Metro UK	Metropolitan Cammell Carriage and Wagon Co. Ltd, Saltley, Birmingham, England
Midland UK	Midland Railway Carriage and Wagon Co. Ltd, Oldbury, Birmingham, England

Interior Designer

* Marquetry made by Albert Dunn in 1920s
(*) Marquetry probably made by Albert Dunn

Car Types

Parlour	Pullman car with 2 saloons, 2 coupé compartments, 2 lavatories
Kitchen	Pullman with 2 saloons, a kitchen and one coupé, 1 lavatory
Parlour/Brake	Pullman with 2 saloons, 2 coupés and a brake compartment, 1 lavatory
S1	Sleeping car with 8 single and 4 double compartments
Luxe	Sleeping car originally with 10 single compartments (most later converted to Luxe 20 in the Depression by adding extra bunks)
Lx 18s	Sleeping car with 9 double compartments, 1 service, 1 lavatory
Lx 18L	Sleeping car with 9 double compartments, 2 lavatories, one extra large
YUB	Sleeping car with 7 double, 4 treble compartments

Where Acquired

WL	Compagnie Internationale des Wagons-Lits et des Grands Express Européens

BRITISH PULLMANS

Carriage	When Built	Where Built	Interior Designer	Type Originally	Type for VS-O-E	Where Acquired	Where Restored	Decoration
AUDREY	1932	Metro UK	G. F. Milne*	Kitchen 20 seats	Kitchen 20 seats	David Lowther	Carnforth	Marquetry landscape panels; Art Deco strip lights
CYGNUS	1951	B'ham UK	Waring & Gillow	Parlour 26 seats	Parlour 26 seats	N. Yorkshire Moors railway	Carnforth	Mahogany panels, mirrors, old prints
IBIS	1925	B'ham UK	Unknown*	Kitchen 20 seats	Kitchen 20 seats	Standard Gauge Steam Trust, B'ham	Carnforth	Greek dancing girls marquetry
IONE	1928	Metro UK	Unknown	Kitchen 20 seats	Kitchen 20 seats	P. W. Whitehouse	Carnforth	Burr wood panels, Victorian frieze
MINERVA	1927	Midland UK	Unknown*	Kitchen 22 seats	Parlour/Brake 26 seats	Lytham Creek Railway Museum, Lancs	Carnforth	Edwardian-type marquetry
PERSEUS	1951	B'ham UK	Waring & Gillow	Parlour 26 seats	Parlour 26 seats	N. Yorkshire Moors Railway	Carnforth	Yellow wood panels, old prints
PHOENIX	1952 (chassis '27)	Metro UK	Waring & Gillow 1981	Parlour 26 seats	Parlour 26 seats	Hotels-Restaurants Mercure, Lyon	Carnforth	Oval frames of marquetry flowers
ZENA	1928	Metro UK	Unknown	Parlour 24 seats	Parlour 26 seats	Terry Robinson	Carnforth	Art Deco Marquetry
Baggage Car No. 7 (957)	1943	LNER UK		Brake van pigeon carrier	Baggage car	W. McAlpine	Carnforth	

CONTINENTAL RAKE

Carriage	When Built	Where Built	Interior Designer	Type Originally	Type for VS-O-E	Where Acquired	Where Restored	Decoration
W–L 3309	1926	Belgium	René Prou	SI	SI	WL	Bremen	Floral Art Deco marquetry
W–L 3425	1929	B'ham UK	René Prou	SI	SI	WL	Bremen	Art Deco leaf marquetry
W–L 3473	1929	Metro UK	Morison(*)	Luxe	LX 18S	WL	Ostend	'Flower Garland' marquetry
W–L 3482	1929	Metro UK	Maple*	Luxe	LX 18S	WL	Ostend	'Trapeze' marquetry
W–L 3483	1929	Metro UK	Morison(*)	Luxe	LX 18S	WL	Ostend	'Flower Basket' marquetry
W–L 3525	1929	France	René Prou	Luxe	LX 18L	WL	Ostend	'Sapelli Pearl' inlay
W–L 3539	1929	France	René Prou	Luxe	LX 18S	WL	Ostend	'Sapelli Pearl' inlay
W–L 3543	1929	France	René Prou	Luxe	LX 18L	WL	Ostend	'Sapelli Pearl' inlay
W–L 3544	1929	France	René Prou	Luxe	LX 18L	WL	Ostend	'Sapelli Pearl' inlay
W–L 3552	1929	France	Nelson	Luxe	LX 18S	WL	Ostend	Tiger-Lily marquetry
W–L 3553	1929	France	Nelson	Luxe	LX 18S	WL	Ostend	Tiger-Lily marquetry
W–L 3555	1929	France	Nelson	Luxe	LX 18S	WL	Ostend	Tiger-Lily marquetry
W–R 4095	1927	B'ham UK	Unknown	Wagon-Restaurant 38 seats	36 seats	WL	Bremen	Black lacquer panels with sporting animals
W–R 4110	1927	B'ham UK	Unknown*	Wagon-Restaurant 38 seats	36 seats	WL	Bremen	'Etoile du Nord' flower baskets
Pullman 4141	1929	France	René Lalique	Pullman-Restaurant 20 seats	37 seats	Aerostock SARL	Bremen	Lalique glass of Bacchanalian maidens
Bar Car 3674	1931	France	Gérard Gallet (1981)	Wagon-Restaurant 56 seats	Bar Car	Private owner	Bremen	Art Nouveau, grand piano
W–L 3912	1949	Belgium		YUB 26 berths	Staff Car 14 berths & baggage	WL	Bremen	Mahogany panels
W–L 3915	1949	Belgium		YUB 26 berths	Staff Car 14 berths & baggage	Aerostock SARL	Bremen	Mahogany panels

[73]

Ione *on the scrapheap*.

Chapter Three

FINDING AND RESTORING THE CARRIAGES

Princess Grace in the Lalique restaurant car, which was eventually bought by the King of Morocco. This Pullman car 4163 was used in the film
Murder on the Orient Express.

O N a torrentially rainy day in the autumn of 1977 Sotheby's organised a sale of Wagons-Lits rolling stock at Monte Carlo goods depot. James Sherwood, who had begun to take an interest in the revival of the Orient-Express at the time of the last run earlier in the year, went there to examine the carriages and perhaps to make a bid. The five carriages had been taken for a joy ride from Nice to Monte Carlo that morning and Princess Grace had eaten brunch in the lovely restaurant car designed by René Lalique. Prince Rainier was there too, as Peter Wilson, the famous auctioneer and head of Sotheby's, prepared to start the sale. The carriages were arranged as a backdrop for the auction and Paul Bianchini, who had liaised between Sotheby's and Wagons-Lits, took his place on the platform. The station was swarming with pressmen and television crews and the coverage was enormous.

Aided and abetted by his railway friends Bill McAlpine and Lord Garnock (once Vice Chairman of British Rail) and supported by Gérard Gallet (who was later to be responsible for the decor of the VS-O-E trains), James Sherwood entered the bidding. He lost the first two cars to the King of Morocco whose agent was buying for the royal train. Luckily they only wanted two carriages and Sherwood took the plunge and bought the next two cars, both sleepers built in 1929. One was built in France and decorated by René Prou and was bought for £41,600 ($72,800), while the other, constructed in England and decorated by Morison, cost £23,400 ($41,000).

Railway cars are very large, long and bulky objects and impossible to park at the bottom of the average garden. Wagons-Lits were happy to transport them – but 'Where would Monsieur Sherwood like them delivered?' Where indeed.... The problems were only just beginning.

The press exposure at the sale convinced James Sherwood that the name Orient-Express had tremendous drawing power and it en-

these rotten, rusting hulks could ever become 'runners' again. The elegant lines were there, but the windows had been smashed, floorboards were missing and the marquetry was so covered with years of grime and filth that the patterns could hardly be seen, let alone admired.

Before deciding exactly what rolling stock was needed it was necessary to plan the VS-O-E route carefully. The most travelled routes in Europe are from London to Paris and Paris to Milan, and the favourite tourist destination in Italy is Venice, which has always had a

ABOVE *Lord Garnock and his locomotive,* The Great Marquess. RIGHT *Bill McAlpine and his locomotive the* Flying Scotsman. *These two men, both noted railway enthusiasts, encouraged James Sherwood and helped him to turn the Venice Simplon-Orient-Express into a reality.*

couraged him to proceed with a project which was gradually becoming more defined in his mind. It was at this stage that I began to be involved. Our travels were suddenly extended beyond ports, container terminals and the latest crane installations. Now we went to freezing and often snowy railway sidings in Spain, Paris, Ostend and Carnforth, near Lancaster, in the north of England. My first railway trip was to Carnforth. I was quite unsuitably dressed for clambering into derelict railway carriages – it was only after I had made three ascents that the staff produced a ladder. It was hard to believe that

LEFT *The sale at Monte Carlo in 1977. James Sherwood is flanked by Gérard Gallet (on his right), Lord Garnock and Bill McAlpine (on his left).*

*After the final run of the Brighton Belle in 1972, Audrey
was preserved by David Lowther, a master at Eton College.*

faithful and devoted following of British visitors, so it was decided to follow this route even if this meant two trains and the complication of the Channel crossing.

The next question was whether the train should go further east, possibly all the way to Istanbul in the track of the old Simplon-Orient-Express. But it was felt that only a very small proportion of the people expected to travel on the train would want to go all the way to Turkey. Early on it was clear that the restoration was going to cost a phenomenal amount of money and that to run the train successfully it had to have a high occupancy, which meant doing the journey at least twice a week. All the way to Istanbul was not possible in the time. It was decided to follow the Simplon-Orient-Express route only as far as Venice using sumptuous between-the-wars carriages previously operated on this route and to use Golden Arrow Pullmans for the journey between London and the English Channel.

Sea Containers started to acquire rolling stock in Europe and in Britain. Bill McAlpine introduced Bill Devitt, a most knowledgeable railway enthusiast, who was seconded to Sea Containers to search for old carriages that might be acquired for restoration. In England most of the Pullmans were in railway museums or privately owned, whilst on the Continent most of the carriages were owned by the Wagons-Lits Company and had been running on, or just recently withdrawn from, the Spanish and Portuguese railways. One of the English Pullmans, *Audrey*, had been bought by David Lowther, a school master at Eton, when the Brighton Belle stopped running in 1972; he had maintained her beautifully. *Zena* belonged to Terry Robinson of Doncaster who had saved her from being burnt and cut up for scrap. Bill McAlpine led us to several of the younger Pullmans that had been built for the Festival of Britain Golden Arrow and the pigeon transporter which is now Baggage Car No. 7. Two Pullmans had been sold to France and were being used as roadside diners. They had to be road-hauled back across France and swung into the ferry to cross the Channel. One got stuck under a bridge in transit.

In the early days of the VS-O-E project it was thought that part of the English train could cross the Channel with the passengers to join the continental rake. The plan was that the English Pullmans would go to Folkestone or Dover, where most of them would be loaded onto a train ferry, cross the Channel and join a continental rake of sleeping cars for the overnight journey to Venice. It would then have been unnecessary to have continental restaurant cars, as the Pullmans would fulfil that function through France and Italy. But, unfortunately, it was not possible to use the English Pullmans on the continent. The gauge of the railway track is the same, but the brakes, buffers, bogies and vestibules are all different from those required by the continental railway authorities. Most important of all was that as some of the English Pullmans are wooden-framed, they would not have met the continental requirement for steel-framed bodywork.

Venice Simplon-Orient-Express Ltd eventually bought 35 cars. There are nine Pullmans and two baggage cars restored for the UK rake; and twelve sleepers, three restaurant cars, one bar car and two extra sleepers for staff and luggage for the continental rake.

Once the cars had been located they had to be carefully inspected for damage and rust. It proved particularly difficult to evaluate the amount of decay within the side panels. The salt used to clear snowy tracks had worked its way up in the panelling, rotting the interior metal sheeting to a rusty lacework which would all have to be replaced. Brakes, electric wiring and bogies had to meet far more stringent safety standards than those in force when the carriages had first been built, or

Phoenix was brought back to England for restoration from Lyon, France, by road – a long and complicated journey. At one point the Pullman became firmly wedged under a railway bridge. The tyres on the transporter had to be deflated to free it.

indeed those under which they had been running until recently. This fundamental engineering was to prove far more costly than the restoration of the interiors.

VS-O-E Ltd was, in fact, trying to do something that had never been done before. Many carriages have been restored and preserved for museums and for limited runs, but no one had ever restored a vintage railway carriage so that it would be permitted to run in a scheduled service, day-in, day-out. This was quite a different project from that normally attempted by railway preservation societies. A railway historian and preservationist said to me indignantly, 'I wouldn't allow anyone to alter the braking system of my cars'. That is of course the correct attitude towards a museum specimen – but a quite useless approach for carriages that have to do six trips across Europe each week. It would probably have been less expensive and it would certainly have been easier to have built new cars – but nothing could be further from the concept of restoring the Orient-Express. Whenever it was possible to refurbish, to restore or to repair, it was done. Only in the last resort was something replaced, and then the replacement was made by craftsmen using the same techniques as those employed in the 1920s. So it was with horror and amazement

Sleeping car 3309 at Madrid in 1979 before being taken to Bremen for restoration.

that I discovered some passengers on the train actually thought the cars were all phoney – built brand new and 'antiqued'. In most cases railway companies have not respected the sanctity of old cars – indeed almost every carriage acquired had been altered in some way to 'modernise' it, by adding more seats or beds or partitions. Some, like the bar car, had been virtually gutted and redecorated with plastic trimmings. VS-O-E Ltd wanted to get as close to the originals as it could, within the confines of modern safety requirements.

As the VS-O-E routing was across three Common Market countries it was necessary for the operation to be based in one of them for legal and tax reasons. It was possible to arrange favourable financing for the project by forming a company based in Britain called Venice Simplon-Orient-Express Ltd. It was eventually financed in the following way: the rolling stock was sold to Cable and Wireless Ltd and then leased back. Cable and Wireless Ltd were able to use the tax allowances and pass some of them back to VS-O-E Ltd in the form of low interest on the capital. The lease-back operation will last ten years and then the effective ownership of the rolling stock reverts back to VS-O-E Ltd.

VS-O-E Ltd began to gather staff to run the train. Colin Bather, General Manager of the Leisure Division of Sea Containers (which also includes the Cipriani Hotel in Venice, the Villa San Michele in Florence, the Lodge at Vail in Colorado and five first-class hotels in the UK with four golf-courses between them) added the train to his other responsibilities. David Bray was responsible for overseeing the complex engineering requirements of the restoration. Claude Ginella, VS-O-E General Manager, was in charge of hiring the staff and organising the service on the trains. The interior design and finish of both trains was created by the brilliant Gérard Gallet, who also designed the china and glasses that are used in the restaurant cars. Gallet decided that, although there were two very different trains with the English Pullmans and continental Wagons-Lits rolling stock, he would use a 'VS-O-E' style for the interior decor of both rakes. For example, certain patterns of upholstery were used in both trains and the china is the same shape, although in the English rake it has brown patterning to match the brown livery, whilst in the continental rake it is patterned with navy blue.

Workshops had to be found that were capable of carrying out the complicated and demanding engineering overhaul and of producing the high standard of internal finish. On the Continent some preliminary work was done at the Irun Wagons-Lits workshop on the

Sleeping car 3483 at Irun in Spain, 1979.

Spanish border which had traditionally altered carriages for service in the Iberian Peninsula (the railways in Spain and Portugal have different gauges from France). Many of the VS-O-E carriages had been inspected there and were still in the local marshalling yards. But eventually it was decided to split the restoration of the continental rake between the Wagons-Lits workshop at Slykens near Ostend, Belgium, and Bremer Waggonbau at Bremen, Germany. Ostend had concentrated on the routine maintenance of sleeping cars for many years and was given the contract for the restoration of the ten Lx-type sleepers with double compartments. Bremer Waggonbau has always specialised in the major repair of day cars, so their workshop was chosen to rebuild the three restaurant cars and the bar car. In addition they restored the two S-type sleepers with single compartments and the two staff cars, as there was no time to have these completed at Ostend.

RESTORING THE PULLMANS AT CARNFORTH

Carnforth was the first workshop to start restoring the carriages, and VS-O-E Ltd built it in 1979. Bill McAlpine owned the Steamtown Museum site and leased VS-O-E Ltd the land. There were craftsmen available in the area (a furniture manufacturer, Waring & Gillow, had closed down nearby in Lancaster). Steamtown was also accessible by rail and George Hinchcliffe, director of the museum, was an expert in restoration. The Sea Containers Group sent up some of its engineers and George Walker became the VS-O-E site manager.

Bogies ready for testing at Carnforth.

Phoenix, Perseus *and* Cygnus *all had to have their original blue asbestos insulation removed before restoration could begin at Carnforth.*

Before work could begin at Carnforth on the British Pullmans a 10,000 square-foot-workshop had to be built. This has a woodworking shop, a French polishing shop (cosily installed inside two old carriages), a drawing office and a sandblasting area. The painting was done inside the huge hangar. All the Pullmans had to undergo an extensive engineering inspection so that they could be put into first-class mechanical condition with a new braking system, new buffers and modern electrical equipment. The Pullmans had been constructed in two different ways. One group was made on a wooden frame with steel or aluminium panels (*Ibis* and *Minerva* and the younger cars built for the Festival of Britain Golden Arrow), whilst the other group was all steel (*Zena, Ione* and *Audrey*). Each car had to be completely stripped down; this took a year for the first cars during the 'learning how to do it' stage. The cars that had been completed in 1951 had been insulated with blue asbestos. Before work could begin the asbestos had to be removed by specialist contractors. Each car was enveloped in a huge plastic cocoon and the asbestos sucked out from all the crevices.

The next stage was to check the bogies (the wheeled undercarriages of the cars). All the original bogies were retained for the Pullmans except for *Audrey*. All the underframes had to be shotblasted to remove the rust and corrosion. *Audrey* and *Zena* had to have false underframes fitted to make them the same height as the rest of the Pullmans. *Audrey* was originally in the Brighton Belle (an electric unit) and she needed new buffers, vestibules and headstocks if she was

Baggage Car No. 7 stripped to its frame at Carnforth.

to be hauled by a locomotive. The cars with wooden bodies had to be very carefully separated from their underframes so they could be fitted with new brakes and electrical equipment and all the wooden surfaces had to be coated with fire-retardant paint. Special trestles were made to take the steel-bodied cars to prevent them from altering in shape during the manoeuvering, as their interiors might be damaged by settling.

The baggage car was an old pigeon-transporter, which had been used in the north of England, where racing homing-pigeons is a favourite sport. The outside was in terrible condition so the panelling was replaced with teak. But alas, the railway authorities stipulated that all external wooden surfaces had to be covered with steel sheeting. So underneath the brown-painted steel-sheathed exterior of Baggage Car No. 7 there lurks a beautiful varnished teak van.

Electric heating was installed in all the British cars. This involved putting electric wires in conduits and made it necessary to lower the ceilings slightly to accommodate the equipment. All the glass had to be changed to specially toughened safety glass, including the glass in the mirrors and in the Pullman lavatory windows. The oval window in the Pullman lavatory is a traditional feature of Pullman design and the antique glass had to be laminated to toughened glass to comply with today's safety requirements. The lavatories are more elegant now than they ever were in the past. Marble was used for the wash-basins and the surrounds were made of panelling that matches the interior marquetry of the car. Margery Knowles created the lovely mosaic floors, with a different design for each loo depicting the name of every car. I always recommend a trip to the loo on the way to Folkestone for a quiet moment of reflection amidst the polished panelling, gazing at Cygnus or Perseus *in terrazzo*.

The interiors of the cars were lined with wooden panelling decorated with veneers inlayed in the most charming marquetry designs. Each interior had to be carefully removed and each part identified to avoid any confusion when replacing it.

Restoring the marquetry was a very skilled job. Some of it had faded, bits of veneer had fallen out and sometimes holes had been dug in the panels to accommodate new fittings. The panelling was often badly scratched and water had damaged the surfaces and raised the inlay. Occasionally a piece of panelling was so damaged that it had to be completely replaced, and this meant matching the old veneers.

Luckily there was Bob Dunn. He and his family live in Chelmsford and form a close-knit working family group, all totally involved in making marquetry. I went to visit them to see how they worked their magic on the filthy, battered panels and changed them into something so special that no one can go through the trains today without marvelling at their skill.

Bob left school at fourteen and was apprenticed to his father who had founded the business in 1898. At that time they lived in London and his father made the marquetry interiors for at least seventy railway cars. The order books for that period revealed that preparing panels for a whole carriage in the 1920s cost between £50 and £70. Bob's father did the original panels in *Ibis*, *Minerva* and *Audrey*, and in the continental restaurant car decorated in the 'Etoile du Nord' style. He almost certainly made the marquetry for sleeping cars 3473, 3482 and 3483 too, as Bob found bills for matching veneers in the old order books.

Bob now has his son working for him, together with his son-in-law, his two daughters and his wife. They have all shared in the restoration work on the train. They begin by washing the veneer free of the accumulated dirt of years. After drying, any loose bits are stuck back on again. The panels were originally supported on blockboard which has often rotted over the years, so this has to be replaced. Missing pieces of veneer have to be matched, if possible with old veneer.

A new oval lavatory window being made for Ione *at Carnforth.*
The original glass was put back, sandwiched between toughened safety glass.

[84]

Carpenters at Carnforth in front of a nearly finished Pullman.

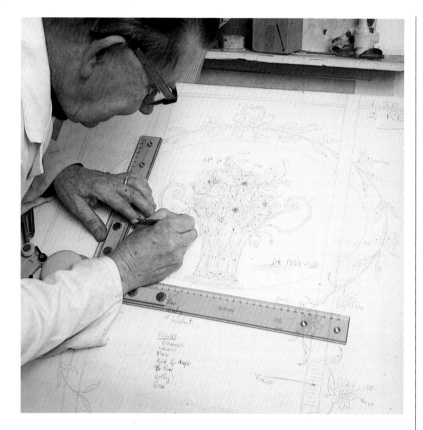

Bob Dunn restored the marquetry panels in the Etoile du Nord dining car 4110. He is working from the original drawings, found in his father's records.

Mrs Dunn shading pieces of veneer by scorching them in a tray of hot sand. This gives marquetry its 3-D effect, particularly well shown in the medallions of Ibis *(see p. 39)*

(Contemporary veneer is cut much thinner and so has to be padded underneath.) Bob had some of his father's original design patterns to work from and could use these as templates when replacing the missing pieces. He also had some of the original veneers in his stock and so could get a perfect match. Several of the oval medallions of Grecian girls in *Ibis* were missing and Bob was able to reproduce them from his father's original plan for the coach. He showed me how he cuts the boxwood veneer for pieces of the Grecian dress, using his 'donkey', slicing the sandwich of wood with his fine fretsaw. Each piece of veneer is sand-shaded, by placing it in a hot sand bath for a few moments. This gives marquetry its '3-D' look, as the scorching makes

shadows on the thin sliver of wood. Then the wood has to rest, to reabsorb moisture, as it has become distorted with the heat. It has to adjust back to its original shape exactly or it will not fit into the final jigsaw. It is tremendously painstaking work and the matching of grain and colour tone in the veneer is really an artistic achievement. It took these skilled craftsmen three weeks to make one of the flower-spray ovals in *Phoenix*.

RIGHT
The marquetry panel completed for dining car 4110.

The Dunns restored the marquetry in *Ibis*, *Minerva*, *Audrey*, *Zena* and *Ione* and also for the 'Etoile du Nord' restaurant car on the Continent. They found that *Audrey* had pieces of glass embedded in the landscape scenes – a result of bomb damage in Victoria Station in 1940. They also made the new panels for *Phoenix*, which were taken from a design by Waring & Gillow found in Bob's father's records. The flower petals were made of boxwood and the centres of sycamore, ramie, walnut and padouk, with pale Brazilian mahogany leaves set in a background that looks like watered silk, but is in fact a superb burred veneer.

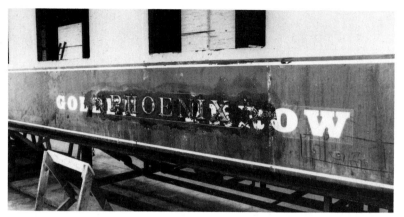

The name Phoenix *reappears as layers of paint are stripped away.*

The finishing touches: marquetry panels for Ione *being French polished at Carnforth.*

After the marquetry panels had been restored by the Dunns they were returned to Carnforth for polishing. Most of the cabinet makers and French polishers had previously been employed at Waring & Gillow's main furniture factory in Lancaster. They had been responsible for restoring the *Queen Mary* and *Queen Elizabeth* after they had served as troopships during the war, but the factory had been closed down in September 1962. When the word got around that VS-O-E Ltd was restoring the Pullmans various craftsmen reappeared, only too pleased that they could use their skills again. At the most active period of the restoration over seventy workmen were working on the VS-O-E project at Carnforth and many others were doing jobs connected with the train off the site.

The French polishers took the panels of marquetry before they were replaced into the cars and built up several layers of shellac on them by squeezing it evenly onto the surface from a pad of cotton-waste, rubbing down between each layer. This has to be done with some sensitivity, as the right amount of varnish brings out the beauties of the veneer, whereas too much obscures the finer detail. The varnishes, like all the paint, have to be approved by the railway authorities as being correctly fire-retardant. Some of the interiors do not have marquetry ornamentation, but are lined with the most lovely burr-wood panels. *Ione*, which has a delightful frieze of roses as its marquetry, has speckled panels of ash as its main decoration. Seasoned wood like this could not be found for her new table-tops so they were made from

Bob Timmins at work on Ione. *He painted the names on all the Pullmans and ensured that the livery was correct.*

wood carefully treated to give the same effect. It is rather sad that these beautiful tables will almost always be covered with table-cloths, as they match the panelling so superbly. The table-tops were not finished by French polishing but had to have a polyurethane lacquer to satisfy the health requirements.

As the engineering and structural work on a car progresses it ceases to look like a skeleton and begins to be clad with flesh again. It is fascinating to see the outside painting beginning. The metal surfaces are carefully prepared and then covered with layer after layer of paint. The whole external appearance changes dramatically from a patched and messy raw metal hulk to a vista of gleaming soft brown elegance, topped with cream above the waist. The coaches are painted in the Pullman livery of 1930, painstakingly researched by Bob Timmins who is quality assurance manager at Carnforth. He devised a special livery for the baggage car and painted all the names onto the sides of the coaches himself, within decorative panels outlined with gold.

Cygnus and *Perseus* were finished first, early in 1981. In a sense they were easier to restore than some of the older carriages but they took longer because the staff were still learning on them. *Ibis*, *Phoenix* and the Baggage Car No. 7 were the next to be completed and these five carriages were exhibited at Victoria Station for the English launch of the VS-O-E in November 1981. It was a tremendously exciting moment for many of the craftsmen who had been working against the clock to get the cars finished in time. Some of them came down from Carnforth to see the beautiful gleaming old carriages. The cars had successfully passed their first trial on 6 October from Carnforth to Hellifield to Carlisle and back to Carnforth (to sighs of relief all round). Now they stood at Victoria, being inspected by enormous numbers of people, surrounded by pressmen and TV cameras. Over 5,000 people walked through the cars in the two days that they were on view. The carriages had become stars again.

Every carriage had to be completely re-wired. Here Zena's *new wiring is being checked.*

[90]

Three sleeping cars at various stages of stripping down and restoration at Ostend.

RESTORING THE SLEEPING CARS AT OSTEND

While the work on the Pullmans progressed at Carnforth, work on the Wagons-Lits cars was started at Bremen and Ostend. Both workshops had previously repaired Wagons-Lits rolling stock, but they were faced with a new challenge as they were not used to repairing such old cars or to producing such a high standard of interior finish.

Ostend rebuilt ten Lx or 'Luxe' sleeping cars. The workshop is in the overall charge of Eric Van Innes, assisted by Maurice Clibouw who has worked for Wagons-Lits for thirty-five years. The VS-O-E site manager was Jack Gotch, who, together with two design engineers and a decor designer, David Miles, was based in Ostend for two and half years.

The Lx cars are of two types: the Lx 18S which has nine double compartments and a service compartment and a lavatory; and the Lx 18L, which has nine double compartments with a standard lavatory and a specially large extra lavatory compartment at one end of the carriage. Before they were altered they were mostly made up of ten double compartments, with a lavatory at one end. The service compartments are used by the steward to prepare early-morning breakfast in the cabins and to serve coffee en route.

The ten Lx sleepers arrived in various stages of disrepair. Three particularly bad ones came up from Irun with holes in the sides and the roof, with the ribs rusted through and the doors temporarily botched together. When the lower outside panels of the coaches were stripped off, it became clear that the supporting pillars had rusted away from the underframe and would all have to be replaced. The overall cost of rebuilding was 70 per cent on engineering and 30 per cent on refurbishing the interior, a ratio few passengers appreciate.

Most of the sleeping cars had to be sandblasted to remove layers of old paint and rust. Sandblasting is sometimes called 'grit-blasting' because it involves hosing a special kind of grit through a nozzle onto the metal surface under great pressure; this knocks off the debris, leaving the steel surface raw and clean and ready to be protected with fresh paint. When the coaches were stripped down the original insulation appeared. One carriage had its roof cavity stuffed with what looked suspiciously like twists of brown paper. This had to be removed and replaced with new non-flammable insulating material. There was one unexpected bonus from the leaking roofs – as they had to be removed it was easier to work on the interiors.

As much of the interior as possible was removed before the engineering work started. All the doors were taken out and stood in racks, carefully labelled. The four Lx designed by René Prou have a number of stylised discs of flowers inlaid in the panelling. The veneer had been cut out in several Art Deco patterns and a creamy-white paste of plaster of Paris used as a filler. This had aged so that it looked like ivory. Over the years the panels had been damaged by coat hangers swinging back and forth and gouged with screw holes to accommodate extra fittings. Often the little flowers had been scratched or had cracked badly and needed repairing. But it was very difficult to match

Newly-restored doors, re-varnished with fire-retardant shellac, stacked in the correct order in the wood workshop at Ostend.

the old-ivory texture with new plaster of Paris, even by touching up with cream paint. All the wooden panels in each car had to be stripped of their old varnish and revarnished with five layers of new, fire-retardant shellac. The carpenters' workshop was full of racks of drying doors and their benches were covered with hundreds of small wooden fittings waiting to be re-varnished and replaced in exactly the right spot. There was a lovely fragrance of mahogany sawdust and shellac. Stripped of their marquetry the carriages became anonymous; they even temporarily lost their numbers before sandblasting.

None of the wiring was considered to be safe by contemporary standards and so every carriage was completely rewired. When the cars were built in the 1920s the wires were tucked in behind the panelling in a somewhat haphazard fashion. Today they are bunched together and threaded through tubes – but it still looks like a cat's cradle during installation.

All the metal parts were unscrewed and taken out for cleaning. The sleeping compartments have an amazing number of fittings to hold the

LEFT Working on car 3544 at Ostend.

glasses and carafe and the lights. Most of the luggage racks were intact (they are very strongly constructed) but they all had to be re-chromed. There are several different patterns of luggage rack. My own favourite is the one in the coaches designed by Nelson (cars 3552, 3553 and 3555) where the marquetry is of delicate tiger-lilies and the luggage rack compliments it with embossed chrome flowers.

The light shades are based on a design by René Lalique called 'Tulip' and they have been used throughout both the English and continental rakes. The shade is made of four interlocked petals in opaque glass, a charming and yet simple design.

Gradually the sleepers were reassembled and started to be recognisable again. They were painted in the navy blue livery of the Wagons-Lits of the early 1930s and the brass numbers and letters were screwed into position on the coachwork. They all had the insignia of the 'Companie Internationale des Wagons-Lits et des Grands Express Européens' with the two Belgian lions and W & L entwined. New mattresses were ordered, the seats were upholstered and the marquetry given a final polish. Carpets which had been woven in England by Firth Carpets of Yorkshire were laid in the cabins and corridors and special dark blue mats were fitted in the vestibules, with the Wagons-Lits logo woven into the fabric.

The pressure was tremendous to finish the work in time for the trial runs of the VS-O-E early in 1982. But it was also essential to complete some cars ahead of time so that they could be used for photography. It was crucial that a brochure was produced about the train by the autumn of 1981 to serve as promotional material for the press and travel agents. So the engineers had glamour added to their daily work with the arrival of models, film crews, lighting experts, make-up men and all the paraphernalia that lies behind the publicity process. It was incredibly cold and uncomfortable for a model lying in a flimsy nightdress, hair artfully disarranged, in the only completed compartment of a gutted sleeping car, looking dreamily out into an active engineering shop.

The first sleepers to be finished were two carriages designed by René Prou (cars 3543 and 3544). They were displayed in Paris, Brussels and Venice. There was a frantic effort to complete the other cars in time for the inaugural run in May 1982 with all the tests and speed trials to be fitted into the tightest schedule. The SNCF (French Railways) were exceptionally helpful during this stressful period.

The workshops at Bremen are immediately recognisable by their huge brick cones standing a hundred feet high, the remains of war-time bomb shelters. I first went there just as they were starting work on the restaurant cars. The first car tackled was Wagon Restaurant 4110 which had been built in England for Wagons-Lits in 1926. It has the lovely 'Etoile du Nord' style marquetry with baskets of flowers made of many-coloured woods. Some panels were badly damaged and were sent to Bob Dunn in Chelmsford. As his father had originally made the marquetry for the car in the 1920s Bob was able to match about 90 per cent of the veneers from his own stock and replaced one panel completely using the original drawings – it is indistinguishable from the others. When we arrived at the workshop we were met by the VS-O-E site manager Pat O'Keefe who showed us the restaurant car stripped out with all the marquetry removed, just left with the bare bones of the skeleton. The site was swarming with people – at its peak a work force of about seventy men was employed there on the VS-O-E restoration. There were men on the roof, men stripping the panels off the outside, men taking out windows, men repairing vestibules, men crawling underneath. As soon as our small group gathered to inspect the shell pandemonium would break out with drilling or welding or bashing with a sledge-hammer. I have always suspected that peace descended as soon as we left. It was cold inside the huge hangar, and I discovered that the one warm place was where the wood is worked. Cabinet makers and varnishers world-wide seem to find cosy spots.

One of the main problems with the restaurant car restoration was that Wagons-Lits had lost many of its records during the war and the original plans were never found. A search was made in the Birmingham Museum Archives which had microfilm of the Birmingham Carriage & Wagon Company records (where two of the restaurant cars were built), but without success. However, this search did lead to a triumph on another score, because the original plans of the sleeping cars were found and these proved a great help in the restoration.

The work at Bremen was inspected by the German Federal Railways to ensure that it complied with the regulations at every stage of the rebuilding. Although it was never intended to run the cars in Germany (apart from moving them from Bremen when they were finished) the railway authorities there inspected them for SNCF (French Railways). It became easier after the first car had been completed as the authorities realised that everything was being done correctly. The job was far more complicated than most people imagine, as every single thing used to restore the cars or to refurbish them had to pass regulations for strength, safety, fire-retardant qualities and so on.

The second restaurant car to be completed was the one which is now known as the 'Voiture Chinoise' (4095). Originally this must have been similar to the 'Etoile du Nord' car as it was made for the same service, but the marquetry was not so distinguished. Gallet decided that the interior was to be lined with black lacquer panels removed from a wrecked car in Madrid. I remember looking at the rather dirty black panels, stacked in one of the workshops and thinking that marquetry would be much nicer – but I was quite wrong. It is such an elegant car now, perhaps my favourite for dining in at night. There were great debates about the colour of the ceiling – should it be black or red or white? Gallet decided on a yellow-cream which looks marvellous both at night and in the daytime. The panels have a black shiny surface in which rather naively drawn animals have been incised and then painted in. There are two spouting whales, flocks of birds, an elephant standing in a pool, monkeys cavorting and alpine sheep, bowed down by curly horns, climbing improbable mountains – a charming if unlikely collection.

The bar car was the next in line for restoration. It had finished its life with a revolting plastic decor. After work had started on the engineering, the interior was completely stripped out and Gérard Gallet designed a new one in Art Nouveau style with mahogany bar, etched mirrors and a grand piano. Every train must have its mystery, and how that piano got inside the car is VS-O-E's.

It was decided to have a third restaurant car. Two had seemed sufficient at the beginning, but now it was felt a spare was needed if something went wrong in one of the kitchen cars (Wagons-Lits had said that this was where most dramas would occur – they were right). A continental Pullman located in the outskirts of Paris became available. It was a rather special car, designed by René Lalique for the Côte d'Azur Pullman and I went along on the inspection trip. When we got to it we found it was locked. While waiting for the key, I wrote down all the numbers, and copied the manufacturer's plaque – I was becoming quite professional. On this visit we noticed that there was an old Wagon-Lit standing nearby, which was also for sale. It was built in the 1940s and was very similar to the type of car used in the James Bond film *From Russia with Love* and it was in good condition. VS-O-E Ltd eventually bought it to be used as a staff car and it was sent to Bremen to be overhauled. There are two staff cars in the continental rake and although they do not have marquetry decoration, the mahogany panelling of the corridors is very beautiful and they fit in well with the older cars. The staff do very long hours on the continental rake and need to have somewhere to catch a nap – also the heavy luggage is stored in the staff cars together with extra linen.

In the Lalique Pullman was a kitchen compartment with a magnificent partition of little wooden cupboards with brass knobs built to hold the china and glass. Beyond this was a depressing mess of cracked windows, dirty curtains, bits of carpet and fold-away chairs. It smelt damp and musty. But on the walls were the Lalique panels of Bacchanalian Maidens, immodestly holding their bunches of grapes. There were six different designs in the long panels, with a frieze above and below of smaller panels. We counted them anxiously, trying to work out how they could be remounted to fit the interior, if it was to be remodelled and the antique kitchen area removed. It was decided, sadly, that the cupboards would have to go as they were quite impractical, blocking the access to one third of the car.

The Pullman and the staff car were sent to Bremen. When the Pullman arrived there the Lalique panels were carefully removed so that engineering work could start. Most of the silvering had come off the backs, or had slithered down into rather messy blotches at the bottom of the panels. They were sent to be resilvered and then stored away until they could be replaced when the coach was ready. I was in Venice promoting the train when we heard that most of the Lalique panels had been stolen from a locked shed at the Bremen works. It was six weeks before the inaugural run.

This was a great blow. Paul Bianchini started a search for other panels (some similar ones had been sold at the Sotheby's sale). We knew that a number of coaches had been decorated in this style and the word went out in 'railway circles'. But we had no luck and although we hoped against hope that the missing panels would turn up, they have not come to light. Perhaps they are tucked away somewhere near Bremen, perhaps they were destroyed when the thief realised they were too 'hot' to handle, or perhaps they are decorating some glamorous bathroom.

The Lalique car could not be ready for the inaugural run, but it was needed urgently as soon as it could join the rake. Gallet decided that

The Venice Simplon-Orient-Express won the 1982 Coachmakers' Award presented by the Worshipful Company of Coachmakers and Coach Harness Makers. The photograph shows James and Shirley Sherwood with the Master of the Company, Major William Hallam Wharfe.

only one half of the car could be decorated with the remaining glass panels and the second section of the car was simply lined with mahogany and mirrors. The car joined the rake in July 1982. Hardly anyone seemed to notice that only one section of the coach had the Lalique panels. One other feature of this car is that the windows are operated by great levers which roll down the whole window, instead of having the small windows at the top which slide apart horizontally.

René Lalique had created the Lalique Glass Company in the 1920s; it still produces the famous sculptures in glass and is represented in all the most elegant and exclusive shops in the world. The Company agreed to look at the possibility of remaking the panels, but warned that casting the moulds would cost a fortune. One panel was to be borrowed from the car to be used as a model and four patterns of panel were prepared for re-moulding. When they finished they were lovely, faithfully copying the original, but the colour did not match the remaining originals. The glass in the carriages had aged over the years and become more yellow in tone. So one compartment of the carriage now has old panels and the other new, the difference noticeable to the discerning eye.

Now that the three restaurant cars are finished and are running with the bar car in the centre of the rake it is interesting to compare them. They are all very different, one with marquetry, another with black lacquer, the third with Lalique panels and the bar car with its Art Nouveau etched mirrors. It is impossible to decide which I prefer.

The effort involved in restoring the cars was far greater than was originally anticipated. The standard required by the various railway companies was far more stringent than when the carriages were first built over fifty years ago, but the tests were passed with flying colours, thanks to the most dedicated groups of technicians at Carnforth, Ostend and Bremen.

The final accolade – although it certainly was not meant as praise – came from a railway expert who said to me, accusingly, 'You've restored the cars so well that you will confuse future railway historians'.

Chapter Four

DESIGN AND ARTEFACTS

A surprising number of objects was needed to complete the trains after the restoration of the bodywork and the interiors had been finished. They included chairs, glasses, cutlery, china, bed linen, towels – the list seemed endless. Fabrics had to be selected to fit with the interiors and they had to have the 'feel' of the 1920s while being fire-retardant at the same time. There were lots of designs in the Wagons-Lits archives and Paul Bianchini selected a number of them so that Gérard Gallet had some authentic guide-lines to follow. The pattern used for the cutlery had been originally designed for Wagons-Lits in 1903, while the china, which has a blue pattern on the continental train and a brown pattern on the English Pullmans, was a modification of an English design of the 1820s with the VS-O-E logo fitted into the coloured scroll-work. The china was produced in Limoges. The silver was copied from Wagons-Lits designs, with particularly pretty bud vases, heavily weighted in the base so they do not topple over when the train is rushing along. Gallet had to produce drawings for champagne buckets, tea pots, silver trays, sugar bowls, cream jugs and serving dishes. The design of the glasses had to be carefully thought out, with a heavily weighted base to prevent spillage. Gallet designed a decanter and seven different shapes and sizes of glasses, all emblazoned with the Art Nouveau VS-O-E logo. These were made in France by Cristallerie. The table cloths were specially woven with the logo and produced in beautiful subtle colours, as well as bedding for the sleeping cars and towels inside the wash cabinets. Gallet produced a second logo in an Art Deco style to

be embroidered on the towels and face cloths and lovely sheets with the logo entwined within a feathery pattern all over the linen. The design of the blankets is similar to the old Wagons-Lits design, but they are very fluffy with satin edges, and again have the VS-O-E logo woven in brown on the cream wool. There are napkins, pillow cases and tray cloths, and small towels on the floor by the bed.

One of the things that people remember best from their earlier journeys on Trains de Luxe are the lamps in the sleeping cars and in the Pullmans. They had usually disappeared from the carriages long before they were bought by VS-O-E Ltd and so it was impossible to furnish the trains throughout with old lamps. But the moulds still existed so new lamps were cast at Best & Lloyd, Birmingham. The same company made the torch-light fittings for the English Pullmans. At one time the Pullman lamps had shades made of potentially inflammable celluloid, but VS-O-E had very pretty pink, red and pale beige-grey shades made of pleated silk which are both safer and more elegant. *Audrey* originally had bright chrome lamps which were quite different from all the other lamps in the English Pullmans, so replicas of this were specially made just to complete her decor. It was fortunate that Ray Towell, the Steamtown works manager, had one in his collection which was copied.

The Pullman chairs were made and upholstered in Yorkshire. Gillian Drury copied the original designs, although the pattern for the dining chairs had to be slightly simplified. They could not be too large as space is very limited in the continental dining cars – it is essential to have dining tables for two and for four people fitting in with a corridor between them if sufficient people are to be accommodated in each car at meal times. The upholstery fabrics were chosen from a selection of eight basic designs, mostly made in Britain by British Replin, Ayr, although the cut moquette velvet used for the continental dining cars

Table setting showing china, glass, silver and linen specially created for the Venice Simplon-Orient-Express by Gérard Gallet, and now on sale as part of the Venice Simplon-Orient-Express Collection.

*Gérard Gallet, who was in overall charge of design
for the Venice Simplon-Orient-Express.*

RIGHT *Paul Bianchini, manager of the VS-O-E Collection,
who was responsible for gathering the artefacts for the train.*

Pierre Fix-Masseau, a leading French poster designer since the late 1920s, creator of a memorable series of posters for the Venice Simplon-Orient-Express.

was made in France. Many fabrics were woven especially for the train and were all fire-retardant. Some of the curtain materials and the fabrics used for the pull-down blinds were sent away to be fire-proofed and this sometimes resulted in a disastrous loss of texture. The fabrics have to be of top quality to stand up to the wear and tear they are exposed to in the trains. Some were very expensive; fabric for the curtains in *Cygnus* cost over £40 per yard.

One of the great pleasures I have had during the VS-O-E project has been learning to appreciate the range of railway posters. The early ones are very delightful, but the ones which have the most impact for me are those of the 1920s and 1930s and two of the most outstanding poster artists of that period were Cassandre and Fix-Masseau. It was decided that the VS-O-E must have some very special posters designed and Paul Bianchini introduced us to Pierre Fix-Masseau. We visited him in his studio in Paris, where he showed us examples of his work including his two most famous railway posters, one for the Côte d'Azur Pullman designed in 1929 and the other called *Exactitude*, designed in 1932. Reproductions of *Exactitude* must be in every poster shop in the world and are shown to every art student as an example of superb design.

Exactitude, *Pierre Fix-Masseau's most famous poster, designed for the French railway company Etat in 1932.*

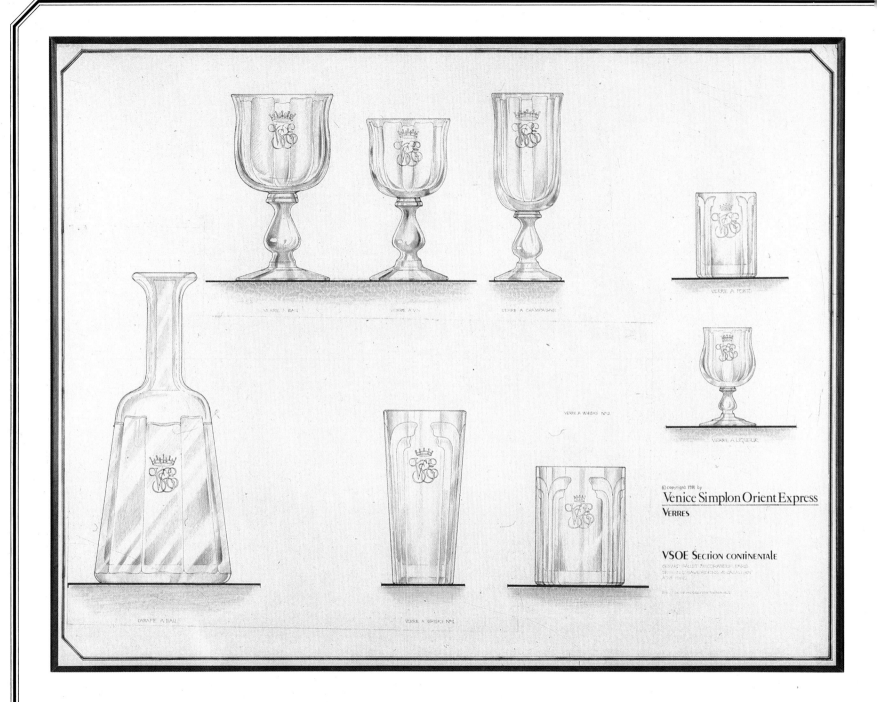

VERRE A EAU   VERRE A VIN   VERRE A CHAMPAGNE   VERRE A PORTO

VERRE A WHISKY N°2

VERRE A LIQUEUR

© copyright 1981 by

Venice Simplon Orient Express

VERRES

VSOE Section continentale

CARAFE A EAU   VERRE A WHISKY N°1

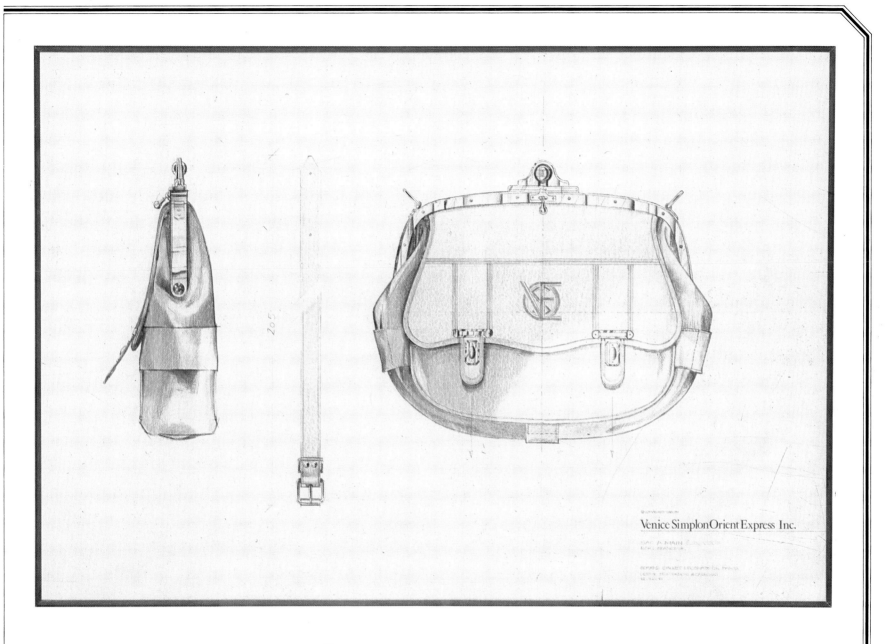

Gallet's drawing for the VS-O-E glasses and the original design for the VS-O-E handbag,
based on the traditional Wagons-Lits ticket collector's bag.

One of the most popular of Pierre Fix-Masseau's posters for the VS-O-E is the girl in the sleeping compartment, now known as the 'madonna' after the heroine of Dekobra's novel, The Madonna of the Sleeping Cars.

Fix-Masseau was intrigued by the proposition and enthusiastically accepted a commission to do a series of posters for the train. He did posters of Victoria Station, Paris, the Alps and Venice and two others showing the interior of a restaurant car and the interior of a sleeping compartment (known by enthusiasts as the 'Madonna'). He was convinced that the Wagons-Lits rolling stock crossed the Channel as the Night Ferry used to, so he painted the train in the Victoria Station poster in the blue livery of the continental rake (he has altered this now). At the time we commissioned him we still thought that some cars would cross the Channel in the ferry, which explains why one poster design is of a ferry boat with some sleeping cars tucked in the hold. Unfortunately this design could not be used as it gave the wrong impression, but I have put it in the book as it is one of my favourites.

Recently Fix-Masseau has done a splendid poster of Milan and another celebrating the centennial of the Orient-Express. He also designed the cover for this book – his first book cover. There has been a great resurgence of interest in his painting and he is having a retrospective exhibition of his work in Paris at the Bibliothèque Nationale in 1983 at the age of 78.

Fairly early on in the Venice Simplon-Orient-Express project it became clear that passengers would want to buy mementoes of their journey. The cost of designing all the items needed to refurbish the train was very high and so it was decided to create the 'Collection Venise Simplon-Orient-Express'. As most of the design work was done in Paris and Gallet and Bianchini lived there, it seemed obvious that the first boutique selling Venice Simplon-Orient-Express mementoes should be based there and that the train should be supplied from Paris. Gallet designed a shop in the rue Boissy d'Anglas with windows to look like those of a brown Pullman coach. Inside, the ceiling is button-padded like the interior of Queen Victoria's drawing-room car and the display cabinets have marquetry panels by René Prou (which had been bought previously at the Monte Carlo auction). The flowered chandelier makes the connection with Venice. The boutique sells china and glass, posters and towels, blankets and linen. The models of Pullmans, sleeping cars and restaurant cars are favourite items and there is a particularly successful ticket-collector's handbag. The opening of the shop was so crowded that it was impossible to see anything of the displays as a thousand people jammed together to celebrate both in the shop and on the pavement. But many of them came back later to have a better look.

VENICE SIMPLON
ORIENT-EXPRESS
LONDON · PARIS · VENICE

Pierre Fix-Masseau's design for a poster showing a train ferry.
This design was never put into production because the original idea of transferring
carriages directly by ferry between England and France proved to be impractical.

Three Logotypes are used to decorate items produced for the trains and for sale. The first, by P. Sharland, is a reflection of Art Nouveau. The second, by P. Stillwell, is based on the designs of René Prou, while the third is a powerful and stylish evocation of the geometry of Art Deco by Gallet. VS-O-E Ltd also has the right to use the original crests of the Pullman Car Company and the Compagnie Internationales des Wagons-Lits et des Grands Express Européens.

PLANNING THE JOURNEY

ONE of the most important parts of planning for the VS-O-E was drawing up the contracts with the various railway companies so that the trains could be hauled across Europe. This involved three major aspects: the route, the timetable and the locomotive power to pull the train. Nagelmackers had a similar set of problems when organising the first Orient-Express, for he too wished to slot his luxury carriages into a system geared to more mundane traffic.

The main routing was decided early on in the project, in 1978, and was from London to the Channel, across to France, then from the coast to Paris, Lausanne, the Simplon Tunnel, Milan and Venice. The first part of the journey followed the route of the Golden Arrow and Flèche d'Or from London to Paris, originally promoted by Lord Dalziel. The second leg, from Paris to Venice, was exactly the same route as the Simplon Express which had started in 1906. This later became the Simplon-Orient-Express by international treaty in 1919 and was organised by André Noblemaire.

At first the plan was to use Dover and Calais as the Channel ports, but passengers would have had to walk a long way from the train to the ferry in Dover, so the choice shifted to Folkestone. The Boulogne authorities agreed to allow the continental part of the train onto their pier at Boulogne, and again this made it very much more convenient for passengers transferring from the ship. A number of elderly passengers were expected among the travellers and VS-O-E Ltd wanted the manoeuvring between ship and rail to be as easy as possible.

Colin Bather, managing director of VS-O-E Ltd, watches Maurice Poinsignon of SNCF (French Railways) signing the contract enabling the Venice Simplon-Orient-Express to operate a scheduled service through France. This ceremony was held on the inaugural run from Venice to London in the Lalique Pullman. The Lalique glass panels shine in the background.

James Sherwood asked Lord Garnock, a keen railway enthusiast and a member of the British Rail Southern Region board, to recommend someone who could open negotiations with the various railway companies. Lord Garnock arranged that General Nigel St George Gribbon of the Sallingbury Company would negotiate for VS-O-E Ltd, supported by Colin Bather and Alain de la Motte, both of whom spoke several languages. In the UK agreements had to be drawn up with British Rail (Southern Region) and with Sealink. The European side of the rail network involved the French (SNCF) Swiss (CFF) and Italian (FSS) railways. It was much more complicated than an occasional charter trip, as VS-O-E Ltd had to organise a regular schedule of three weekly return trips across Europe and at least two return trips within England. It was absolutely essential that the timetabling brought the passengers to the right place at the right time without the haulage charges pricing the project out of existence. Although Sea Containers had already bought a number of coaches for the VS-O-E and placed them at the various railway repair shops, the expensive restoration could not go ahead in a vacuum. A number of times it looked as if the whole project would have to be called off. The final 'go-ahead' decision was made as late as the summer of 1981 when James Sherwood, having looked at all the figures, telexed Colin Bather: 'After the various cost reductions and adjustments are made, my basic decision is to go ahead. We must make every effort to make a success of the venture. . . . It's all systems go and let our prayers be answered.'

The timetabling was critical to the VS-O-E project. The train had to leave London about noon and give passengers lunch on the way from Victoria to Folkestone; this timing was very tight, less than one and a half hours. The transfer to the ferry and the Channel crossing would take about three hours (but the time on the Continent is

CIES DES CHEMINS DE FER DU NORD-DE PARIS A LYON ET A LA MÉDITERRANÉE -
DE BERNE A NEUCHÂTEL - CHEMINS DE FER FÉDÉRAUX ET DE L'ÉTAT ITALIEN
Cie INTLE DES WAGONS-LITS ET DES GRANDS EXPRESS EUROPÉENS

ÉTÉ 1906
SIMPLON-EXPRESS

BERNE

LAC LÉMAN

MILAN

TRAIN DE LUXE
ENTRE
(LONDRES) CALAIS-PARIS-INTERLAKEN
(LONDRES) CALAIS-PARIS-LAUSANNE-MILAN

ZERMATT ET LE CERVIN

BERNE

POUR RÉSERVER SES PLACES A L'AVANCE S'ADRESSER AUX
AGENCES DE LA COMP. INTERN. DES WAGONS LITS

*Poster by Henry Mouren for the Simplon-Express which
started in 1906 after the opening of the Simplon Tunnel.
It went from Paris to Venice and was very popular with honeymoon couples.
It became the Simplon-Orient-Express in 1919 when the route
was extended to Constantinople.*

generally one hour later than England) so passengers board the continental rake at about 5 p.m. The journey between Boulogne and Paris takes about five hours which would leave time for an elegant meal. This was important because some people would want to get off in Paris and passengers would be boarding there as well. If the train reached Paris by ten in the evening, boarding passengers could join a second sitting in the dining cars before going to bed. On this timetabling the train reached Lausanne at 5.30 a.m., ready to take on a load of fresh croissants for breakfast and the morning newspapers. Early risers could see the Matterhorn and go back to sleep during the Simplon Tunnel. Milan was scheduled for just after 9 a.m. (convenient for businessmen travelling from Paris) and after brunch on the train, the VS-O-E would arrive in Venice at 1 p.m. This arrival time was dictated by the problems of vacating rooms in Italy, as no one is obliged to leave an Italian hotel room until one o'clock in the afternoon. But if the train arrived in Venice later in the afternoon there would be a terribly short turnaround time for the return journey. It had to be there by 1 p.m. to allow a departure at 5.30 p.m. It takes several hours to clean and re-provision the train, to fill it up with water, for the staff to take a breath and a shower and to change into fresh uniforms.

The return trip, from Venice to London, also had a number of critical timings. The first sitting of the evening meal had to start before Milan, so that people boarding there could join the second sitting. Again, the leg from Milan to Paris was organised to suit a business traveller who might choose to take the train in the evening rather than cope with a fog-bound airport. A good meal in lovely, unique surroundings would contrast pleasantly with the 'herded-like-cattle' aura of most plane services today and arrival in the centre of Paris would be 8.30 a.m., an appropriate time for the businessman. It was decided to provision in Paris and so the early morning stop there would take some time – re-watering, re-provisioning, sorting out the on-coming passengers. The sleeping compartments just recently vacated by the overnight travellers would have to be cleaned quickly to make them ready for the Paris to Boulogne leg of the journey.

The next problem was the turnaround of the continental rake at Boulogne. This was a complicated cross-over. Continental passengers left to go over on one ferry which passed another ferry southbound in the Channel containing the next group of VS-O-E passengers going to Venice. The continental train had about three hours to be cleaned and

Claude Ginella, general manager of the Venice Simplon-Orient-Express.

to take on a new team of staff. Boulogne was to be 'home-base' for the continental rake and its staff, while Paris was to be the 'provisioning centre'.

The traveller returning to England would reach Folkestone early in the afternoon, have a leisurely tea on the UK rake coming into Victoria at about 5.30 p.m., and still be in good time to reach a hotel and have an evening 'on the town' in London.

The real question-mark over the operation was whether the turn-arounds at the end of each leg were going to work. How reliable were the ferries going to be? If the VS-O-E was delayed by bad weather in the Channel or snarls in the railway system, could the lost time be made up? What about the railway unions' penchant for strikes at holiday times? The UK part of the journey was relatively simple, as it was a much shorter leg, but the continental rake covered 900 miles from Boulogne to Venice and had a really tight schedule.

In retrospect no-one had appreciated how crucial the ferry service would be. In the first year of operation there were a number of ferry breakdowns and delays, including the holing of one ferry on rocks in Folkestone harbour. The ferries went on strike for a short time and the British Rail unions struck for sixteen days in July, less than two months after the service had started.

As the first year progressed and the staff became more experienced, the turnarounds became highly organised and worked amazingly well. The original plan had been for two London-Venice return trips and one Paris-Venice trip per week, but in the autumn of 1982 the demand for seats became so great that it was decided to fit in three return trips from London to Venice, and these were organised so that the train was serviced for one day a week in Boulogne. The servicing involves a work force of about thirty men.

This timetable had to be fitted into the complex network of services running both on the Continent and in Britain, and also connected by ferries over which VS-O-E had no control. It would have been better to go more slowly on certain parts of the route, and it would have been nicer to have some of the track in better condition, but these are difficult factors to influence. It took three years of negotiation to organise the timetable that is now in use.

In the early days of planning it was hoped to have part of the route steam-hauled. The only possibility was from Boulogne to Amiens, where the track is not electrified. It would have been marvellous as well to have had the train emerging majestically from Victoria Station shooting steam in all directions on the inaugural run. But it was not to be. VS-O-E was denied permission to steam haul out of Victoria for safety reasons and all negotiations for steam-hauling in France proved abortive – either the locomotives were not powerful enough to pull such a heavy train (over 900 tons) or the price demanded was incredibly high (£18,000 or $33,000 per trip). It would also have added another two hours to the time taken from Boulogne to Amiens. So, sadly, the idea had to be abandoned.

The staffing on the British and continental rakes was approached differently. The British Pullmans are staffed by Travellers Fare (the catering wing of British Rail). They wear uniforms designed for the VS-O-E and must be the most photographed railwaymen in the world.

The staffing of the continental train presented a number of problems. Although it would have been attractive to hire ex-Wagons-Lits staff, most railway staff with experience of luxury trains were over fifty and it was anticipated that the continental journey would be very exhausting with its two long legs (from Boulogne to Venice and Venice to Boulogne in forty-eight hours) with a short turnaround time at

VENICE SIMPLON-ORIENT-EXPRESS TIMETABLE

		Friday	Saturday		Sunday		Monday		Tuesday		Wednesday		Thursday
		S	S	N↑	↑N	S	S	N	↑N	S	S	N↑	↑N
LONDON (*Victoria*)	D	11.44			17.17	11.44			17.36	11.44			17.36
FOLKESTONE (*Maritime*)	A	13.15			15.40	13.15			15.40	13.15			16.00
	D	14.00			14.40	14.00			14.40	14.00			14.40
BOULOGNE (*Maritime*)	A	16.50			13.50	16.50			13.50	16.50			13.50
	D	17.44			12.40	17.44			12.40	17.44			12.40
PARIS (*Austerlitz*)	A	22.29			08.47	22.29			08.47	22.29			08.47
	D	22.46			08.30	22.46			08.30	22.46			08.30
VALLORBE	A		04.22		02.53		04.22		02.53		04.22		02.53
	D		04.47		02.25		04.47		02.25		04.47		02.25
LAUSANNE	A		05.21		01.48		05.21		01.48		05.21		01.48
	D		05.27		01.40		05.27		01.40		05.27		01.40
BRIG	A		06.56		00.04		06.56		00.04		06.56		00.04
	D		06.59		00.02		06.59		00.02		06.59		00.02
DOMODOSSOLA	A		07.31	23.30			07.31	23.30			07.31	23.30	
	D		07.48	23.05			07.48	23.05			07.48	23.05	
MILAN (*Central*)	A		09.15	21.30			09.15	21.30			09.15	21.30	
	D		09.40	20.57			09.40	20.57			09.40	20.57	
VERONA (*Porto Novo*)	A		11.12	18.53			11.12	18.53			11.12	18.53	
	D		11.20	18.48			11.20	18.48			11.20	18.48	
VENICE (Santa Lucia)	A		12.52	17.25			12.52	17.25			12.52	17.25	

S = Southbound from London   N = Northbound from Venice

Venice. It was decided to hire young men with hotel rather than railway experience, who would bring a fresh enthusiasm to the job as well as youthful energy. They all had to speak several languages so that they could communicate with the varied passenger nationalities. Claude Ginella had to hire and organise the train staff and create a kitchen to service the continental train.

It was decided to do the laundry in Paris. Paris has always been famous for its laundry services – in the days of the rubber boom in South America the rich rubber barons sent their linen back from the Amazon to Paris to be laundered.

Drawing showing the uniforms worn by Wagons-Lits staff before 1914.

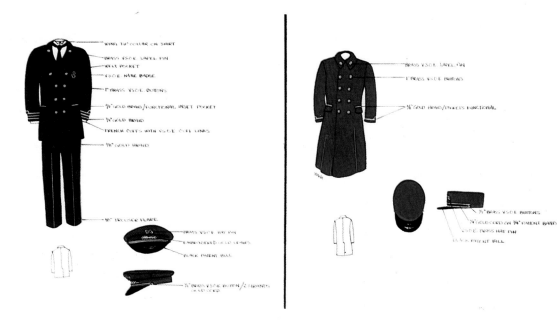

Two uniforms for the Venice Simplon-Orient-Express: on the left the Train Manager of the English Pullmans and on the right the Cabin Attendant for the continental rake. All the uniforms were specially designed using the pre-1914 styles of the Wagons-Lits Company as models.

[111]

Staff group showing the uniforms worn by the continental train and kitchen personnel. The Chef is Michel Ranvier.

The positioning of the kitchens used for preparing food for the train was very important. Originally Boulogne seemed the obvious place, but Claude Ginella was keen on Paris as the food markets there are particularly good, so eventually the kitchens were built in the Gare d'Austerlitz. Provisioning the train is complicated. As the train passes through northbound in the morning all the food for brunch is put on board, as well as the food for the return dinner that evening between Boulogne and Paris. At the evening stop in Paris food and supplies for the trip to Venice and back to Paris are taken on board. The train stops at Lausanne for fresh croissants early in the morning in both directions and can take on a few fresh supplies in Venice and Milan. Storage space is at a premium and cooking on the train presents similar problems to cooking on a yacht, working in a very confined space and with considerable movement and vibration at speed. Everything has to be properly stowed or it comes adrift and gets broken. On the day every week when the continental rake is serviced at Boulogne the provisions are sent by van from Paris to Boulogne during the morning.

One of the most important appointments was the Chef, Michel Ranvier. He had worked at the famous *Frères Troisgros* and *Restaurant Jamin*, and has prepared some wonderful meals in the restricted surroundings of the train's kitchens. Originally the idea was to have a number of alternatives for the main course – but space and time made this difficult. He changed the menu several times during the first year, adapting it to suit the varied clientèle. He was familiar with French tastes, but discovered, for example, that some Americans were appalled by their introduction to sweetbreads, which are considered a great delicacy in Europe. Here are some examples of his menus:

SUMMER DINNER

Le Gâteau de Légumes au Homard Breton
et sa Compotée de Tomates Fraîches au Basilic

La Natte de Sole au Beurre de Pomerol
et sa Tagliatelle de Carottes et Courgettes

Le Petit Rôti de Veau et sa Sauce à l'Oseille

La Sélection du Maître Fromager

La Poire Pochée au Vin Rouge
et son Sorbet aux Mûres de Framboisier

Les Mignardises

AUTUMN DINNER

La Fricassée d'Ecrevisses et de Langoustines
au Caviar servie dans son Marmiton

L'Elégante 'Saint-Jacques' cuite dans sa
Coquille aux Herbes Fines

Les Noisettes de Chevreuil Renaissance
nappées de leur Sauce poivrade
aux Baies de Genièvre

La Sélection du Maître Fromager

La Charlotte aux Marrons glacés d'Automne
et la Crème de Caramel blond

Les Mignardises

The staff on the continental rake number forty on each run, which includes four chefs, four assistant chefs and four washers-up. There is one cabin attendant to each sleeping car (eleven in all), a cleaner and one technician to repair faults, a train manager and a restaurant manager, plus maîtres d'hotel, wine stewards and waiters. There are three teams of staff during the peak season, each doing one return trip a week. At least another 100 VS-O-E staff are 'behind the scenes', manning the reservations, the repair workshops, the kitchens in Paris and the administrative organisation.

Pardon me boy, is that the Venice-Simplon choo-choo?

(Marketing 11 February 1983)

TRAVELLING CHIC ON THE ORIENT EXPRESS

(Daily Telegraph 17 April 1982)

Orient Express Rolling Again in Art-Deco Luxury

(International Herald Tribune 26 May 1982)

Champagne fuelled the train

NIGEL DEMPSTER
ON THE ORIENT EXPRESS

Travelling isn't murder on Orient Express

(Travel Trade Gazette 4 June 1982)

glamorous train of thought

(People 3 February 1982)

BUMP! went Lady Kilmarnock in the middle of the night

(Daily Mail 27 May 1982)

The second age of the train of romance

(The Scotsman May 1982)

THE RETURN OF THE ORIENT EXPRESS

The king of trains (and the train of kings), in regal splendor, prepares to roll again from London to Venice

(Signature January 1982)

Passion on the Orient Express

(News of the World 22 August 1982)

RESTORING THE ART OF TRAVEL

(Railway World May 1982)

Orient Express back 'on profitable lines'

(Daily Telegraph 11 November 1981)

Return of the Orient-Express

LA RECHERCHE DU TRAIN PERDU

(Town & Country April 1982)

ERIC NEWBY TAKES THE WAGON-LIT TO VENICE

DREAM TRAIN FROM PLATFORM 8

(Observer Review 30 May 1982)

A touch of class

(Rail Enthusiast December 1982)

The Once and Future Train

Europe's fabled Orient Express returns in pristine splendor

(Time 30 August 1982)

MR SHERWOOD CHANGES TRAINS

(Harpers & Queen February 1982)

Chapter Six

PROMOTION AND THE FIRST RUNS

AMES SHERWOOD had a very clear idea of the image he wanted for the Venice Simplon-Orient-Express. It was to suggest an experience of special quality, unusual, exclusive and luxurious, evocative of a time when travel was glamorous and perfect service was taken for granted. The theme became 'we have restored the art of travel'.

Promotional material had to be available by the autumn of 1981 at the latest in order to launch the train and to start regular services by May 1982. Work started on a brochure and a film in the summer and promotional tours were planned by VS-O-E Ltd to market the train in the USA and Japan. Public displays of completed carriages were also planned in a number of European cities, backed up by trial runs. The climax of the campaign was to be the inaugural run from London to Venice on 25 May 1982 with film crews in attendance.

THE BROCHURE

Work was started on both the brochure and the film in the summer of 1981, long before most of the cars were finished. As a result all the visual material had to be created from the three cars that were available for photography at that time. The brochure was a very important part of the promotional campaign as it was essential for travel agents and journalists who could not see the train for themselves, giving them a clear impression of the train and of the experience of the journey. The Vernon Stratton Agency was commissioned to prepare the brochure and at the same time work started on the film.

What kind of clothes should the models in the brochure wear? The pictures needed a period feel without being theatrically 1920s, so the girls were dressed in soft flowing clothes and the men wore bow ties. In a desperate last-minute search for some suitable accessories to clothe his bit players, Vernon Stratton went to a little shop in Ostend where

A promotional film and a brochure advertising the train had to be made at an early stage, well before most of the cars were fully restored. Photographers and models had to work in the cramped conditions of partially completed cars in cold and draughty workshops and still create an illusion of luxury, comfort, elegance and style.

he discovered a cache of old velour hats. The shopkeeper could hardly believe his luck when Vernon bought them all – they had been sitting on the shelf since pre-war days.

The Pullman *Cygnus* was ready in Carnforth and sleeping car 3544 at Ostend. The third car completed at that time was in Bremen, the 'Etoile du Nord' restaurant car. These cars had to be brought to life and filled with glamorous people. The accoutrements of the publicity machine had to be taken to the three workshops and models filmed in seemingly elegant surroundings while apparently travelling, eating and sleeping in a moving train. All the camera's tricks and illusions were brought into play. Cars had to be specially mocked-up; the sleeping car had half a compartment removed so that the cameraman could peer through more easily at the lovely model lying 'asleep' on the couchette clad in a flimsy nightdress, suggesting a gently seductive mood, but actually gazing out into an active engineering workshop. The workforce loved it. . . .

When the shots of the dining car were being prepared one part of the coach was still incomplete so the photographers were able to capture the happy scene more easily. It was a bizarre sight as one third of the car was just bare frames and timbers, whilst the rest had chairs and tablecloths and linen with models sitting looking perfectly composed, enjoying a wonderful meal as if they were racing through the French countryside rather than shivering at Bremer Waggonbau.

For the shots of the outside of the sleeping car, two cars were taken to a station near Ostend in the middle of the night so that they could be filmed without interruptions. Everything was prepared – the lights softly glowing inside the cabin windows, the arc lights outside correctly balanced, the model walking along the platform – when suddenly a 'real' train tore into the station and a whole group of back-packing students swept onto the platform, surrounding the two gleaming old cars and the exasperated film crew. Filming had to start all over again.

The pictures were designed to evoke an air of mystery: an elegant girl sitting in a cabin by herself writing a letter, gazing dreamily out of the window; a handsome young man casting a roving eye round the dining room; or a beautiful older woman graciously engaged in conversation with her dignified beau. Details of other cars were added to the films that had been shot at Bremen, Ostend and Carnforth to show the medallions of Greek dancing girls from the Pullman *Ibis* and the particularly beautiful marquetry from the René Prou S-type sleeping car. Pictures of London, Paris, Milan and Venice were inserted to chart the route of the train through Europe, interspersed with some of the posters Fix-Masseau had created for the train.

The brochure, complete with route map and details of the timetable, was finished in October for the Victoria launch and in time to be posted to travel agents world-wide at the beginning of the publicity campaign.

THE FILM

The film made by Purchasepoint was a brilliant juxtaposition of still pictures mingled with movie film, designed to give a more detailed impression of the journey than could be given in the brochure. Virtually everything had to be done with only three completed cars, but luckily it was possible to include shots of the Pullmans during one of their speed trials. Introduced by an exciting sequence of the Orient-Express leaving Istanbul, a clip borrowed from the film *Murder on the Orient Express*, accompanied by a haunting soundtrack, the film was also completed in time for the Victoria Station presentation.

DISPLAYS

The first time the restored carriages were shown to the public was at Victoria Station on 11 November 1981. *Perseus*, *Ibis*, *Phoenix*, *Cygnus* and Baggage Car No. 7 had arrived in London the day before and were stored overnight at Stewarts Lane Depot. It was a very exciting moment when I saw these vintage carriages coming slowly into view and drawing up majestically at Platform 8, as in the glamorous days of the Golden Arrow. On the first day they were on display to the press and travel agents who turned up in force, walking through the Pullmans admiring the new cutlery, china and glass. Everything had been prepared so that the cars would look at their best both inside and out. On the next day the Pullmans were open to the general public and the news quickly spread. On an icy-cold November day people queued right round Victoria Station to see the train. Some enthusiasts queued for up to three hours and 5,000 people walked through the carriages. There was massive coverage in the newspapers and on TV and radio. The train was news!

The public showings of the continental train were planned for the early spring of 1982. The first was in Paris on 9 March when a splendid dinner party was given at the Gare d'Austerlitz, the event crowned by a truly magnificent cake.

The continental carriages were first shown to the public at the Gare d'Austerlitz, Paris, in March 1982. A grand dinner party was held on the platform beside the train. The high point of the evening was the cutting of a magnificent cake by the actress Charlotte Rampling.

The next presentation which was in Brussels, the original home base of Wagons-Lits in the nineteenth century, turned out to be exciting in a number of unanticipated ways. It started well with a presentation of the film in the Astoria Palace, a wonderful old hotel in the centre of the city which has a famous railway bar with splendid Pullman chairs and marquetry panelling from old Wagons-Lits cars. After the reception the party went down to the railway station in veteran buses accompanied by a descendant of Georges Nagelmackers who is a director of Wagons-Lits. A substantial crowd was beginning to form, but there were hardly any Belgian police to marshal them.

Two cars were floated on barges across the Basin of St Mark's to be moored outside the Cipriani Hotel for a promotional party.

The platform became extremely congested as the coaches could be approached from across the lines and hordes of people were storming in from four different directions. Several thousand people tried to get into the carriages in an amazing mêlée that almost became a riot. Some climbed in through the windows, others thumped on the outside demanding to get in. It was most alarming for the staff trapped on the train. Amazingly very little damage was done except for a few scratches to the paintwork. It was an awesome demonstration of the crowd-pulling potential of the train.

There were several presentations in Italy in the spring, the most visually exciting being the show in Venice. This was a magical moment. Two cars, one the 'Etoile du Nord' restaurant car, the other a Wagons-Lits sleeping car, were cautiously run onto two railway barges and towed through the Basin of St Mark's to be floated alongside the Cipriani Hotel. Small bridges linked the two barges so that visitors could walk from the Cipriani through the cars and then back onto dry land again. The presentation started at the Cini Foundation on the island of San Giorgio Maggiore where the Mayor of Venice came to wish the venture good luck. Back at the Cipriani there was a band playing and everyone danced. Three hundred guests had been invited to view the carriages, more than 450 came, and most of them walked through the train at least twice. It was like a fairy tale to have these magnificent coaches floating on the Lagoon in Venice. Three days later they were gone, on a trial run from Venice to Florence, partly to test the cars, and partly to show them to the Sea Containers Group boards of directors who had been meeting at the Cipriani. They had authorised the expenditure of millions of dollars, so we took them on the train itself for a preview. During this trip the first meal prepared in the restaurant car was served, and James Sherwood and the Chef happily signed the menus for the guests.

PROMOTIONAL TOURS IN THE USA AND JAPAN

Promoting the train in the USA was a different project. Obviously the train itself could not be shown. A frenetic roadshow across the USA started in the early part of 1982. The tour lasted two weeks and included visits to New York, Philadelphia, Boston, Washington, Miami, Palm Beach, New Orleans, Denver, Houston, Los Angeles, San Diego, Santa Barbara and San Francisco. Our punishing schedule was made worse by the time of year. Snow was falling along the East Coast, and flying was difficult. We landed at Washington the day after

an airliner had crashed into a bridge while trying to take off in appalling weather. The Government had closed its offices for the day due to the storm, but still a number of hardy adventurers braved the snow to see the presentation.

The mechanics of the roadshow were complicated. Invitations had been sent out in advance to journalists and travel agents. Two teams of technicians and public relations people leap-frogged from one place to another. Our morning would start early with a breakfast conference for journalists. Later there would be a reception and perhaps lunch and a showing of the film, supported by a display of posters, uniforms and a Pullman place-setting with glasses, cutlery and tableware. After lunch it was on to the next town in time for a hurried cup of coffee and the evening presentation. When that was finished we often went on to yet another city to sleep.

At each presentation journalists asked innumerable questions of extraordinary diversity. James Sherwood was constantly giving interviews on local television and radio networks, while I fielded questions on the history of the carriages, their restoration and how they were equipped. David Picken, who headed the American sales team for VS-O-E Ltd, was swamped with travel agents grabbing posters for their window displays. We had a good response from the local press and magazines began to fill up with articles about the train. Often people tried to make reservations on the spot and at one lunch in San Francisco I managed to fill a whole carriage with friends.

The Japanese are train mad and it was decided to promote the train in Tokyo during a trip to the Far East. The presentation was held at the elegant Okura Hotel. The film dubbed into Japanese was particularly well received. At this presentation a Japanese film director arranged to film the train during its trial run for one of the prime-time television travel programmes in Japan. The British ambassador blessed the proceedings.

TRIAL RUNS

As the carriages were completed they were tested at speed to ensure that they would meet all the safety regulations required by British Rail and the continental railways. The Pullmans were first tested on 6 October 1981, hauled from Carnforth to Carlisle on the Scottish border and back. To everyone's relief they passed with flying colours. Fortunately, subsequent trials both in England and on the Continent were equally successful. The first passenger trip was a special Pullman

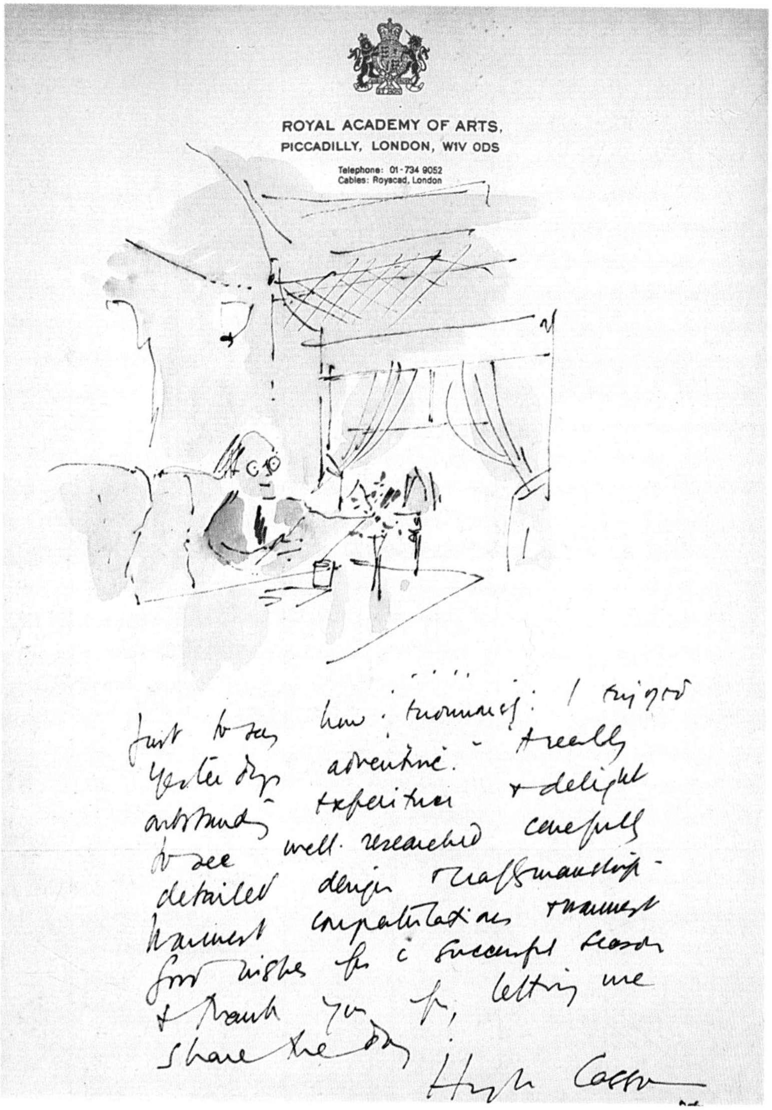

ROYAL ACADEMY OF ARTS,
PICCADILLY, LONDON, W1V 0DS

Telephone: 01-734 9052
Cables: Roycad, London

Just to say how enormously I enjoyed yesterday's adventure – a really astonishing experience + delight to see well researched carefully detailed design + craftsmanship. Warmest congratulations + warmest good wishes for a successful season + thank you for letting me share the day

Hugh Casson

The first trial run with passengers was a special journey from Victoria to Brighton to celebrate the opening of the Brighton Festival. Sir Hugh Casson, the President of the Royal Academy, wrote this letter to say how delighted he was with the trip.

run from London to Brighton to open the Brighton Festival. On a beautiful morning on 28 April 1982, the special guests gathered at Victoria Station, admiring the gleaming Pullmans which included *Audrey* for the first time. It was a particularly fitting occasion for she was returning to the route on which she had served for so many years, the Brighton Belle. The passengers included Paul Channon, the Minister for the Arts, Sir John Tooley, the Director of Covent Garden, and Sir Hugh Casson, President of the Royal Academy. Lunch was served on the way down and a classic strawberries and cream English tea on the way back. Paul Channon opened the Festival at an exhibition of Picasso's work for the theatre, which included set and backdrop designs for Diaghilev's ballet, *Le Train Bleu*.

The most important trial was the first complete journey all the way from London to Venice and back to London again. Cars were being rushed to completion at Carnforth, Bremen and Ostend with workshop staff working round the clock to finish them. Vital pieces of equipment were being raced between Ostend and Bremen, with dramas at the customs on the Franco-Belgian border. Amazingly, on 11 May 1982, everything was ready with *Zena* and *Minerva* just down from Carnforth. The train was jammed with photographers and camera crews and as it left Victoria Station film crews hovered overhead in helicopters.

All went smoothly to Folkestone and across the Channel. At Boulogne the continental train was waiting, a truly magnificent sight, with all seventeen cars assembled in the rake for the first time. Everyone climbed into their compartments and collapsed as the train left, with champagne flowing. It is hard to describe the excitement, jubilation and exhaustion of that moment. Seeing all those beautiful carriages reassembled in their gleaming splendour was almost incredible after such long preliminary wrangles with workshops and railway authorities. It was the most overwhelming moment for me during the whole of the restoring of the train. We'd done it!

Dinner was served to us in the 'Voiture Chinoise' which I had last seen in pieces at Bremen – it looked quite wonderful. Dinner was very elaborate and took a long time to serve. This was a dress rehearsal for the staff, who were learning how difficult it is to serve a dining car packed with hungry people. For some of them it was their first experience of pouring wine in a confined, vibrating space. Some of the kitchen racks had not been completed and glass and china was sliding around in the small galley. Chef Ranvier had prepared an elegant meal

James and Shirley Sherwood in front of Zena *before leaving Victoria on the trial run to Venice on 11 May 1982.*

which was complicated by a problem with the gas supply. The gas kept turning itself off and could only be turned on again when the train was stationary. Despite all the problems the kitchens produced a fabulous meal and eventually we all returned to the bar car to sing around the piano. Billy Hamilton, in charge of public relations, found himself in wonderful voice with his repertoire of 1920s numbers.

What had been learnt from this trial trip? First of all, it was obvious that the staff cars had to be in the centre of the train, and not at each end, where they had been placed in the trial run. There simply was not time for staff to walk through half the train to shave or get a change of clothing. Second, the kitchens had to be reorganised with far more anchor points and storage space. The gas problem had to be solved. The young staff needed more training and experience, although there was no doubt about their enthusiasm and excitement for the job. Finally, to give more space in the cabins, passengers should be advised to bring only easily manoeuvrable luggage into the compartments – they should check heavy cases through to Venice in the baggage van.

The inaugural run of the Venice Simplon-Orient-Express left London with its first paying passengers on 25 May 1982. Several factors had influenced the choice of date, particularly the imminent visit of the Pope, who was arriving in Britain on 28 May. The Falklands War seemed at one time to threaten the whole launch, but because of the number of people involved it was decided that it would be wrong to cancel or postpone it at such short notice.

The inaugural run of the Venice Simplon-Orient-Express left Victoria on 25 May 1982. Among the celebrities was the actress Liza Minelli.

The band of the Coldstream Guards on the platform at Victoria.

From early in the morning on 25 May, a bright sunny day, Victoria Station was packed with people in 1920s costume, photographers and a fine array of veteran cars. Champagne was flowing freely, and continued to do so for the next twenty-four hours. The band of the Coldstream Guards was playing vigorous martial music. Alan Whicker and his team from Yorkshire Television's *Whicker's World* were making the feature film on the train's inaugural run that was to be shown on British television on New Year's Day 1983 (it was seen by nine million people). The platform was decorated with palm trees and the whole atmosphere was extremely friendly, lively, sparkling, noisy and exciting. Shortly before the time for departure James Sherwood mounted the stage in front of *Audrey* and gave a speech which was televised all over the world. He declared, 'The Venice Simplon-Orient-Express is resumed'. There were numerous journalists on board, including Michael Demarest from *Time Magazine*, who was very interested in the details of the train's restoration and did two more journeys to check what later trips were going to be like (his two-page spread reached 26 million people later in 1982); Eric Newby, known for his travel books and passion for trains, wrote a marvellous article in the *Observer*; Betty Kenward, who meticulously reported for *Harpers & Queen* under the pseudonym of *Jennifer*; Julian Pettifer for the BBC who had to phone through his report from the Cipriani, and Nigel Dempster, the gossip columnist, extracting the unexpected from the rich and famous.

There were titles galore. The Duchess of Westminster with her sister and bodyguard, Princess Esra Jah, Earl Jermyn, Lady Denise Kilmarnock, Sir Peter and Lady Parker. All the board of the Sea Containers Group had flown in from Spain, Hong Kong and the USA. Bill McAlpine saw where his encouragement had led us and the (Pullman) Millers from Chicago came in memory of his grandfather, George Pullman.

Sir Peter Parker, Chairman of British Rail, and Lady Parker on the inaugural run in Perseus.

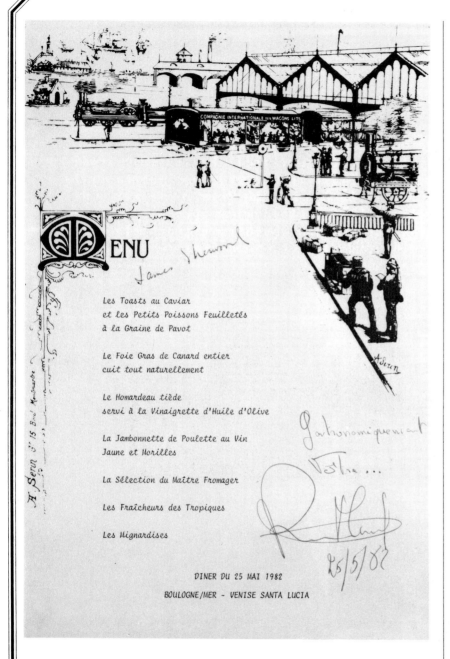

ꝈENU

James Sherwood

Les Toasts au Caviar
et les Petits Poissons Feuilletés
à la Graine de Pavot

Le Foie Gras de Canard entier
cuit tout naturellement

Le Homardeau tiède
servi à la Vinaigrette d'Huile d'Olive

La Jambonnette de Poulette au Vin
Jaune et Morilles

La Sélection du Maître Fromager

Les Fraîcheurs des Tropiques

Les Mignardises

*Gastronomiquement
Votre...*

25/5/82

DINER DU 25 MAI 1982

BOULOGNE/MER - VENISE SANTA LUCIA

The inaugural menu for dinner signed by Chef Michel Ranvier and James Sherwood.

Alan Whicker interviewing on the ferry for his television programme,
Whicker's World.

At 11.44 a.m. prompt the guard blew his whistle and the gleaming Pullmans set off for Folkestone. Lunch was complicated by interviews and cameramen – it was an unnerving experience having every mouthful recorded for posterity. At Folkestone Harbour we boarded the ferry *Horsa*, complete with Palm Court orchestra and more champagne. At Boulogne the long continental train was waiting, with another orchestra and a group of Breton girls in traditional lace headdresses. Slowly the train moved out, sent on its way by the Mayor and a great crowd of photographers and well-wishers. Everyone on the train dressed for dinner. The meal, prepared by Michel Ranvier, was a tour de force. After dinner the bar car became the centre of activity, with the pianist playing until five in the morning. Breakfast was served in the compartments, with fresh croissants brought onto the train at Lausanne. The train passed through northern Italy and reached

Milan, where some revellers from the previous evening tentatively emerged from their compartments. A magnificent brunch was served in the Lalique Pullman car and then shortly after 1 p.m. the train pulled into Santa Lucia Station, Venice, just a flight of steps above the Grand Canal. A band of gondoliers, bouquets of flowers and a bevy of photographers were on hand to greet the train, and the passengers then dispersed to sample the delights of Venice. We went slowly down the Grand Canal, across the Basin of St Mark's to the Cipriani, savouring our return to this most beautiful of cities. It is surely the most magical city in the world and I never return to Venice without a thrill of excitement nor leave without a touch of sadness – the visit is always wonderful but too short.

'Jak' comments on the inaugural run in the London Standard.

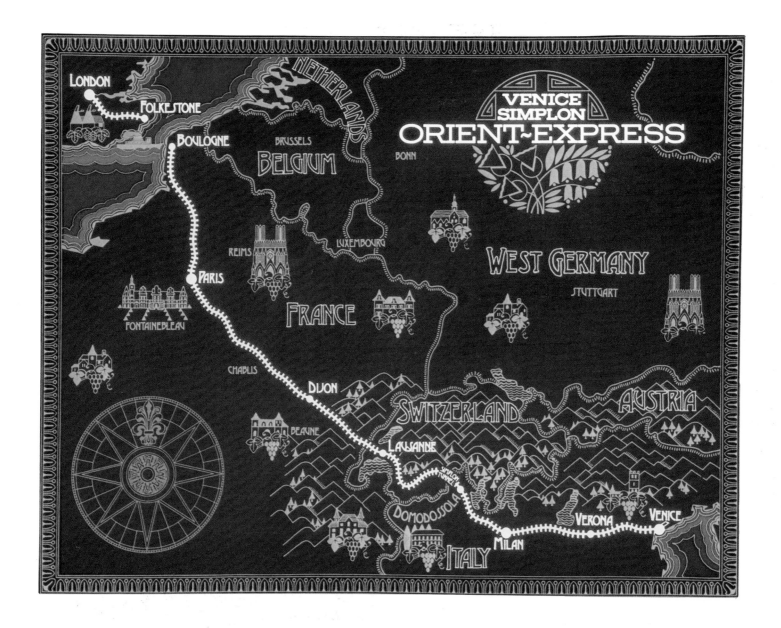

Chapter Seven

THE JOURNEY

THE journey starts at Victoria Station, Platform 8. One of the joys of travelling by train is that you can arrive at the last minute, but I always advise people to get there in good time so that they can walk through the British Pullmans before the train sets off.

First the tickets are sorted out at the Venice Simplon-Orient-Express desk. Luggage for Paris, Milan or Venice is checked in and overnight bags are tagged with the passengers' cabin numbers on the continental train: they will be placed there by the VS-O-E staff at Boulogne. All that passengers need keep by them are their tickets, passports and something warm to wear on the ferry.

The Pullmans come slowly into Platform 8, usually about three quarters of an hour before departure. They contrast vividly with all the other carriages in Victoria Station. The train manager shows the passengers to their coaches where they can settle down and have a glass of champagne. But please, don't just sit there – now is the time to walk through the train. Go right to the end of the platform and climb into *Minerva* which is usually the last coach. She is a traditional brake van with the original braking gear in the last vestibule. She has charming small compartments (coupés) and Edwardian marquetry. *Ione* and *Ibis* also have an Edwardian feel to their marquetry with a frieze of roses and ovals of Greek dancing girls. *Audrey* (ex-Brighton Belle) and *Zena* are most distinctively Art Deco and *Cygnus*, *Perseus* and *Phoenix* each have a style entirely their own. Look into the loos as you pass by: each mosaic floor illustrates the name of the carriage. Read the history plaques in the vestibules and finally admire Baggage Car No. 7, which used to transport racing pigeons.

Poster of Victoria Station by Fix-Masseau.

traditional jointed rails go diddly-dum, diddly-da. By the time the first course of lunch is served the countryside is opening up and the train carves through a chalk cutting in the North Downs to race through Sevenoaks and Tonbridge into the Weald of Kent. This lovely area of wooded hills, known as the Garden of England, is particularly beautiful in spring when the great orchards are in blossom and there are young frisky lambs in the fields. There are lines of very tall poles, covered with hops later in the year. In the autumn the hops are dried in the distinctive conical oasthouses and added to beer to give the traditional 'bitter' taste.

I have had some lovely lunches on the British train. The staff from Travellers Fare (British Rail) are practised at serving three courses in fifty-five minutes, quite an achievement in a vibrating train. Lunch usually starts with a soup such as celery with Stilton cream. Then I have had salmon with tarragon or turkey breast stuffed with walnuts and tiny cranberry tarts, served with fresh, unusual salads and followed by rather sinful desserts such as Tipsey cake, chocolate pots or caramelised tangerines with brandy-snaps. Sometimes I have room to finish with English cheeses and coffee. Prue Leith, who does the catering, has been briefed to make the lunches light, fresh and very British, as a contrast to the elaborate French dinner on the continental train.

Alan Pegler, UK Assistant Train Manager, at Victoria.

Lunch on the way to Folkestone in Cygnus.

The train moves majestically out of Victoria Station at 11.44 a.m. precisely. It crosses the Thames almost immediately and goes past the Art Deco chimneys of Battersea Power Station. Now is the time to concentrate on important things – a drink and the beginning of lunch – as the southern suburbs of London are not particularly inspiring. Listen for the different noises made by the train; *Ibis* is especially vocal going round corners and *Minerva* feels her age at times; there is an even hum on the continuous welded main-line track, but the

The Pullmans going across the harbour bridge to Folkestone Marine Station.

Folkestone is just after the chalk hills of the South Downs. The train reverses down a steep incline and across the harbour into Folkestone Marine Station. Sailing boats and small fishing smacks are moored on either side of the bridge with a view of the White Cliffs of Dover stretching into the distance. The train stops and everyone gets out, sometimes rather reluctantly – I always love the Pullmans and wish that part of the journey was longer.

One of the compartments on the continental train by day (car 3544, designed by René Prou).

The checked luggage is taken out of the baggage car by the porters and loaded straight onto the ferry and from there onto the continental train. The passengers go through passport control to the Sealink ferry waiting by the quay. It could be *Hengist*, *Horsa* or *Vortigern*, all named after early British tribal chiefs, or the *Lord Warden*, a name derived from the traditional title of the head of the Cinque Ports. On the ferry passengers can use the reserved lounge or they can explore the ship. It is fun to watch the ship being cast off from on deck. Slowly the quay slips away, and the ship leaves Folkestone behind, dwarfed by the White Cliffs. In the distance there are some circular Martello towers and the old military canal, part of the extensive network of defences erected early in the nineteenth century when Napoleon was expected to invade England. To the east, up on the cliffs is the imposing mass of Dover Castle.

An hour and a half ahead lies Boulogne. The outline of the thirteenth-century ramparts comes into view and the tall dome of the Basilica of Notre Dame can be seen on a clear day. Boulogne has had a turbulent history, alternating between French and English rule through the Middle Ages. When Napoleon planned to invade England he stationed 160,000 troops there. It was a British Army base in World War I and during World War II it was virtually demolished by the British and Americans before the Normandy landings in 1944. Today it is a ferry and train terminal and a fishing port with many different ships in the harbour.

The large hawsers are thrown ashore, the French dockhands loop them over the bollards, and the ferry comes slowly alongside the quay where the Continental train is standing. A long curving line of elegant blue and gold cars greets the passengers as they walk down the gangplank from the ferry; a magnificent sight. The train cannot be approached directly as the formality of French customs and passport control has to be passed through first, and these lie on the other side of the train. The passengers are shown to their compartments which at this stage are made up for day use with a couch with cushions and head rests and a cabinet containing a washbasin, soap, toilet water and towels embroidered with the VS-O-E logo. Inside the cabinet is a handpainted motif reflecting the marquetry decoration of the compartment. The cabin attendant of each coach collects his passengers' passports. He will organise the customs formalities at each frontier crossed during the night and return the passports before the train reaches Venice.

On board the continental train at Boulogne.

The train, hauled by two diesel locomotives, moves slowly over the harbour pier. As it leaves Boulogne behind it gathers speed along the track which runs parallel to the coast for some miles. There are sand dunes, marshland and low rolling hills interspersed with typical French farm-houses and the occasional small country house. Near Le Touquet is the Forest of Crécy. This famous battlefield has changed little since that day in 1346 when King Edward III of England and his son the Black Prince overcame the might and chivalry of France, through the accurate shooting of the English and Welsh archers. At Abbeville the railway crosses the River Somme and stays beside it as far as Amiens. The Somme was the site of some of the fiercest fighting of World War I but long before this, Henry V forded the river with his army, defeating the French at the Battle of Agincourt in 1415.

In the bar car.

Preparing dinner in the tiny galley.

The first sitting for dinner is now under way in the three dining cars; each is memorable in different ways: the 'Etoile du Nord' car with its marquetry, the 'Côte d'Azur' with its Lalique glass panels and the 'Voiture Chinoise' with its black lacquer panels. I am often asked what people should wear for the trip. My answer is, 'If you feel like dressing in a twenties style – marvellous!'. It is fun to dress up for dinner as one would for an elegant restaurant. The dining cars certainly provide the most beautiful surroundings that one can imagine for a superb meal. I usually wear a head band, a long string of pearls and swank a feather boa. There are generally some men wearing dinner jackets and a few ladies in long dresses, but it certainly is not essential.

Dinner is a splendid affair. Michel Ranvier is one of the great exponents of *nouvelle cuisine* and although I have included some menus elsewhere, they can only give a faint idea of the delicious variety and quality of the food. He starts with wonderful *foie gras*, or with tiny morsels of seafood delicately encased in a sea-urchin's shell, or with lobster in an earthenware pot resting on a bed of seaweed, with the prettiest fresh water crayfish peering over the side. The next course might be sole cooked as a plait (I suppose three strips of fish are braided before being cooked) in a delectable white butter sauce with a scattering of red caviar or a few redcurrants. On another occasion I prised open scallop shells to find a selection of mussels and shellfish nestling inside. Following this was a fillet of young venison or tender veal, served with wild mushrooms and a Madeira sauce. The cheese and desserts are equally delicious and inventive. All the dishes are prepared in the tiny galleys and the standard achieved is really amazing.

At Amiens there is a pause while the double-headed diesels are changed for electric locomotives. On leaving Amiens the line turns southwards, passing through the small town of Boves, which was the most southerly point reached by Henry V in the fifteenth century, and later was the site of a fierce battle during the Franco-Prussian War in 1870 – the war that upset Nagelmackers' early plans for railway routes across Europe. In April 1918 the final German offensive reached this far, stretching the Allies to their limit.

As the train gets nearer Paris it passes through the royal forest of Chantilly, crossing the Grand Canal by a viaduct. The château has long been a centre of French horse-racing and the famous Grande Ecurie was built there with room for 250 horses and their grooms. Louis XIV came to stay in 1671, bringing with him an enormous entourage of 5,000 courtiers.

The first sitting for dinner on a summer evening.

Nearing Paris the landscape becomes more enclosed and wooded. The train stops briefly near Villiers-le-bel-Gonesse where it enters the network of lines converging on the 'Ceinture' – the belt of railway tracks that go all round the city, linking the various stations. The 'Ceinture' runs through the suburbs, but in the distance there are tantalising glimpses of the Eiffel Tower and the dome of the Sacré Coeur. At one point the train crosses two loops of the River Marne, giving a quick view of the forest of Vincennes and the royal château which was enlarged in 1652 by Cardinal Mazarin for Louis XIII. The train passes slowly through the huge marshalling yards at Villeneuve-St-Georges, a principal target for British and American bombing raids during World War II (some of the Venice Simplon-Orient-Express cars were stored there at that time) and runs for a while along the Seine before reversing back along the river bank and into the Gare

Passengers joining the train at Gare d'Austerlitz in Paris.

As the train speeds southwards from Paris, the second sitting for dinner is under way in the 'Etoile du Nord'.

d'Austerlitz. Dating originally from 1843, Austerlitz was completely rebuilt in 1867 to serve as the principal station for the International Paris Exhibition of that year. In 1870, when Paris was besieged by the Prussians, Austerlitz was used as a balloon station. The huge gas balloons became the only means of communication between Paris and the rest of France and were inflated under the station canopy.

At Austerlitz more passengers join the train, and essential servicing is carried out during the short stop. Leaving Paris, the train follows the course of the Seine for a while, passing through the sites of other royal forests while passengers who joined at Paris leave their compartments and make their way to the restaurant cars for the second sitting of dinner. Those who have finished gravitate towards the bar car, where

Paris by Fix-Masseau.

the pianist continues playing into the early hours. By now the compartments are made up into their night-time configuration. The settee is pulled forward and opened out, the upper bunk is erected, and the beds are made up with the elegant sheets and blankets decorated with the VS-O-E logo, with a ladder leading to the upper bunk.

During the night the train passes through Dijon, the capital of Burgundy. After crossing the Saône at Auxone the train starts to climb steadily up to the Franco-Swiss border at Vallorbe, 2,953 feet (900 metres) above sea level. The train stops briefly at Lausanne at 5.30 a.m. to collect fresh croissants and the newspapers. It runs along the shore of Lake Geneva which can be a wonderful sight in the early morning in the summer with the dawn breaking over the mountains. At the edge of the lake stands the Château de Chillon half surrounded by water. The château was immortalised in Lord Byron's poem *The Prisoner of Chillon*, which describes the fate of the Prior of St Victor de Genève who was imprisoned in a dungeon below water level for six years. The line follows the river Rhône southwards, climbing steadily up the Rhône Valley. The foaming waters of the Rhône rush past the track feeding a network of canals to the vineyards in the valley. This is a wintersports area with mountain railways and ski lifts.

I like to order breakfast early so that I can have it while I am watching the Alps. The cabin attendant brings a small tray with thermos flasks of tea or coffee, and with croissant, brioche and the *Herald Tribune*.

The next place to look for is Sion where there are two fortresses perched on peaks overlooking the valley. There were always close connections between the Valais region and the Vatican and in 1506 the inhabitants were given the privilege of guarding the Pope, wearing a special uniform designed by Michelangelo. This privilege is still in force today, and the traditional Swiss Guards are one of the most familiar sights in the Vatican.

Just before Brig the curiously shaped peak of the Matterhorn, 14,690 feet (4,477 metres) high, comes into view to the east. It was first climbed in 1865 by a young Englishman, Edward Whymper, but the ascent was marred by tragedy as several members of the party fell to their deaths when a rope parted on the way down. The train climbs steadily up towards the Simplon Tunnel, passing through Visp and Brig where it sometimes stops for a few minutes. Eventually Brig may be used to connect the Venice Simplon-Orient-Express with ski resorts.

After dinner the staff prepare the silver for the next day.

The passengers return to their cabins and prepare for the night.

Dawn breaks on the Matterhorn.

The Alpine barrier between Switzerland and Italy is pierced by the Simplon Tunnel. One of the epic engineering feats of all time, the tunnel is twelve and a half miles long and took eight years to complete. BELOW *Digging the tunnel.*

Now the train plunges into the Simplon Tunnel, one of the greatest engineering feats of all time. Its length of twelve and a half miles (20 km) makes it the longest rail tunnel in the world and it is 6,890 feet (2,100 metres) below the surface at its deepest point. The Simplon Tunnel marks the transition from the bleak north-facing Alpine scenery to the brilliant southern slopes that sweep down to the fertile plains of northern Italy. The Simplon Pass, crowned by the famous Benedictine hospice at the 6,000 feet mark (1,830 metres), has always

The start of tunnelling operations at Iselle on the Swiss side in 1898.

been an artery for north-south European travellers since the Roman legions surged through in search of lands to conquer. Napoleon ordered the construction of a road across the Simplon Pass to secure his lines of communication to Italy. Completed in 1805, this road was up to 26 feet (8 metres) wide, and was engineered to avoid any gradient steeper than 1:10. The idea of a Simplon Tunnel was encouraged by the successful construction of the Mont Cenis, Gotthard and Arlberg tunnels. In addition, the reluctance of the French to pass through German territory following the humiliation of the Franco-Prussian War of 1870–1 supplied the political will for such a project. However, it was ultimately the governments of Switzerland and Italy, not France, which helped to make the tunnel a reality by subsiding the cost. After long preliminary investigations work finally began on the north side on 1 August 1898. The tunnel was dug simultaneously from both ends, along a course plotted by indirect triangulation, as the great height of the mountain made it impossible to use the normal method of sinking shafts from the surface along the line of the tunnel. Two parallel tunnels were dug, one a pilot tunnel to supply ventilation, power and drainage to the main tunnel. The main tunnel was initially shored up with timber supports and then filled in with a solid brick core around which further enlarging was done in successive stages. When the tunnel had reached the required dimensions the final lining was installed and the brick core removed. Despite previous experience

of mountain tunnels, the engineers building the Simplon encountered many wholly unexpected problems. Water was one of the major obstacles. A total of 242 springs were found, and many delays were caused by torrential flooding. Even worse were the floods of scalding water heated to as much as 50° centigrade (120° fahrenheit) by the temperature of the rock so far underground. In 1904 these hot floods brought work to a standstill for a period. It was only by constantly spraying ice-cold water at high pressure onto the rocks that bearable working conditions could be achieved. Other problems included the crushing pressure of the mountain itself, which kept destroying the wooden support frames 2.8 miles (4.48 km) in from the Italian side. Even at the very end there was a disaster. On the last day, when only about $16\frac{1}{2}$ feet (5 metres) of rock remained between the two teams, an explosion released floods of boiling water and clouds of poisonous gas, killing two engineers. At last, on 28 February 1905, the tunnel was completed. It had taken 2,400 days to build and 1,520 tonnes of dynamite. The work had cost the lives of sixty-seven men.

The track was laid during 1905. It was electrified from the beginning, even though some trial runs were made with steam haulage. On 19 May 1906 the tunnel was officially opened with ceremonies and festivities in both Switzerland and Italy. It was originally single track, with a short stretch of double track in the centre to allow trains to pass, but in 1922 the second tunnel was opened alongside.

Poster showing the new route through the Simplon Tunnel from London to Italy.

It is still a most important tunnel. During periods of political tension it is always well guarded, its security reinforced by Switzerland's traditional neutrality. The greatest threat to it was in 1944 when the retreating Nazis decided to blow it up. Luckily, Italian partisans were able to remove the primed explosives before any damage was done. Even today both tunnels are checked daily by four men, each walking through half a tunnel in four hours. Normally they find nothing more than blind mice and crickets, but on one occasion they met a former Swiss Papal Guard riding through on a bicycle. They knew he had escaped from an asylum because he was riding without lights on the quickest route to Rome. . . .

Emerging from the Simplon into the Italian sunshine at Iselle, the train begins its descent to the plains, stopping briefly at Domodossola to change engines. Domodossola has a curious connection with Scotland. In 1525, following the defeat of Francis I by Charles V at the battle of Pavia, south of Milan, the French king was taken prisoner and his army dispersed. Francis had a personal bodyguard of Scottish archers who tried to make their way back to France. After crossing Lake Maggiore they aimed for the Simplon, hoping that this route would not be watched by Charles's Spanish troops. They left Domodossola along a valley which became impassable with snow and they were trapped for the winter. By the time it thawed they found they liked the area and decided to settle, gradually losing their identity through intermarriage. About fifty years ago their remote valley was opened up by a new road. Local parish registers were found to contain many Scottish names slightly blurred by time, and linguistic experts discovered that some of the local vocabulary had Gaelic origins.

Nearly everyone is awake to see the magnificent scenery of the Italian Lakes, skirting the shore of Lake Maggiore. The scenery is absolutely lovely with the lake and the Boromean Islands set off against the background of the snow-capped Alps, glistening in the early morning sun. Along the lake shore are a number of small resorts, including Baveno, much favoured by Queen Victoria who spent most of her winters abroad in her old age. A royal railway carriage was kept at Calais, ready to speed Her Majesty on her way southwards attached to a suitable Grand Express. At Arona the train leaves the lakes and enters the great Lombardy plain. The scenery is less interesting as agriculture gives way to the industrial approach into Milan, Italy's largest city, and commercially its most important too. The train enters the magnificent terminus of Milan Central, the largest railway station in Europe, at about 9 a.m.

On leaving the Simplon, the train runs into Italy along the shore of Lake Maggiore.

The first girder for the train shed at Milan Central was erected in 1929, weighing 800 tonnes. Milan Central is the biggest railway station in Europe.

The train at Milan under the huge canopy of girders.

The opening of the Simplon Tunnel made Milan the hub of the newly centralised railway network, and on 29 April 1906 the first stone of the central station was ceremonially laid by King Victor Emmanuel III. Railway development in Italy came to a halt in 1914 and it was not until 1921 that work on the station actually got under way. At first, hampered by lack of funds, it progressed very slowly, but from 1925, with the impetus of the new fascist government, Milano Centrale began to take shape. The designer, Ulisse Stacchini, altered his plans several times and in the end he produced a massive monument to so many years of endeavour. The scale of the conception was immense and no expense was spared in its creation. It was inspired by a Roman bath with the entrance formed by a Roman triumphal arch. It contains a variety of splendid ornamental rooms, including vast arrival and departure halls, a Royal Pavilion built originally for the exclusive use of the Italian royal family, restaurants and bars and even a large dormitory for soldiers in transit. Marble, majolica tiles and enormous bronze lights make the interior immensely imposing, contrasting with the powerful utility of the vast train shed whose iron ribs span over 236 feet (72 metres). The architecture itself is a curious mixture of Beaux Arts and Art Deco styles, which are meant to reflect both the spirit of classical architecture in Italy's heritage and Italy's emergence as a modern nation. The building is decorated with powerful Art Deco figures cast in ferro-concrete, the new material of the age. When it was finally completed in 1931, the Italian fascists took pride in having inspired this enormous building, claiming that they stood for national regeneration linked to the glories of Italy's past. After all, Mussolini did make the trains run on time.

The train stops at Milan for about twenty minutes. It is best to check with the train staff – I was nearly left behind on one occasion – but a visit to the huge echoing halls at the front of the massive station is really worthwhile if there is time. As the train leaves Milan Central, reversing back out of the great arched shed, look back out of the window to see the five huge arches receding into the distance.

Brunch is served between Milan and Venice since by the time you reach Venice it is usually too late for lunch. It is served in the Lalique Pullman car and consists of a wonderful selection of hot and cold dishes ranging from scrambled egg with truffles, pasta, fresh-water shrimps, foie gras and cold rare beef, to the most delicious chocolate cake or fresh fruit tart. I remember one gateau of Kiwi scattered with translucent pomegranate that looked too beautiful to eat.

Poster of Milan by Fix-Masseau.

squares and the small, empty churches. Visit San Giorgio Schiavoni where Carpaccio painted a frieze which has St George killing a very bizarre dragon, his most celebrated work. Nearby is the church of San Giorgio dei Greci, which was built by the Greek community in the sixteenth century and has a wonderful collection of icons in the church and in the museum next door. Walk up to the Arsenale, the ship-building centre of Venice from the twelfth century when the city produced a galley a day. In that period the craftsmen worked from scale models which are preserved in the Naval Museum. There are so many places to visit that a good guide book is essential, so I have listed the ones I find most useful in the bibliography.

One of the great pleasures of Venice is the delicious food. The markets have a great range of fruit, vegetables and seafood from the Lagoon and the Adriatic. Pasta comes in every shape, size and colour; Tagiolini verdi gratinati is my favourite, or perhaps a sea food risotto – it is hard to choose.

The Basilica of St Mark's during an aqua alta.

LEFT *The steps outside Santa Lucia Station lead to the Grand Canal.*

An aerial view of the Cipriani Hotel in the foreground, with the Campanile of St Mark's across the water.

There are a number of special occasions in Venice when the city is dominated by local festivals. The historical regatta in September brings out all the old barges crewed by oarsmen in medieval costumes in a splendid procession up the Grand Canal. The Vogalonga is a marathon held in May in which about 2,000 boats participate. They all line up between the Salute and the Giudecca, completely blocking the waterway for ordinary traffic. When the gun goes off the incredible flotilla of small rowing boats moves forward to race to Torcello and back (35 km). Venetians do not jog, they practice for the Vogalonga. Then there is the Redentore in July, when a huge pontoon bridge is erected from the Church of the Redentore to the Zaccharia and the faithful walk across the Giudecca Canal to the church. The most spectacular 'happening' of all is the Carnevale in February. The city is filled with thousands of costumed revellers, the palazzos are opened for masked balls and there are parties every night, culminating with dancing in St Mark's Square. The costumes are remarkable for their variety and originality and it is uncanny to see Venetians in eighteenth-century dress crossing the Grand Canal by gondola – going to work.

Eventually it is time to leave Venice. But the adventure of the great train lies ahead. The excitement of climbing on board the Venice Simplon-Orient-Express at Santa Lucia compensates for the inevitable sadness when leaving this marvellous city. Another wonderful journey is about to start.

The Piazzetta San Marco at Carnival time.

PEOPLE INVOLVED WITH THE VS-O-E PROJECT

INITIATING THE PROJECT

James Sherwood
Lord Garnock
Hon. W. McAlpine
Paul Bianchini

ARRANGING THE ROUTE AND CONTRACTS

Route
James Sherwood

Negotiating for VS-O-E
Colin Bather, *VS-O-E*
Alain de la Motte, *VS-O-E*
Maj. Gen. Nigel St G. Gribbon, *Sallingbury Ltd*

British Rail
James Evans, *BR/Continental Railways Liaison*
Jack Bedser, John Yoxall, *BR/VS-O-E Liaison Officers*

France (SNCF)
Maurice Poinsignon, *Adjoint au Directeur Commercial Voyageurs*

Switzerland (CFF)
T. Schneider, *Commercial Passenger Traffic Manager*

Italy (FS)
Dott. M. Venturi, *Capo dell'Ufficio Centrale Traffico Viaggiatori*

Sealink Ferries
Alan E. Branch, *Commercial Development Manager*

RESTORING THE COACHES

Carnforth
George Walker, *VS-O-E Site Manager*
George Hinchcliffe, *Managing Director, Steamtown Railway Museum Ltd*
Ray Towell, *Works Manager, Steamtown Railway Museum Ltd*
and many highly skilled craftsmen working on the project and engaged by Steamtown Railway Museum Ltd

Ostend (Wagons-Lits workshop)
Jack Gotch, *VS-O-E Site Manager*
Eric Van Innis, *Wagons-Lits Factory Manager*
Maurice Clybouw, *Wagons-Lits Works Manager*

Bremen (Bremer Waggonbau workshop)
Patrick O'Keefe, *VS-O-E Site Manager*
H. Ambrosius, *Works Manager, Bremer Waggonbau*

ENGINEERING

David Bray, *Sea Containers Group Vice-President, Engineering*
Mick Clitherow, *Sea Containers Group*
Andre Segond, *VS-O-E, Continental Maintenance & Engineering Design*
Alan Ackroyd, *Consultant Engineer*
A. Vialatoux, *Chef du Département Entretien du Matériel Remorqué, SNCF*
J. Strebelle, *Inspecteur Principal, Direction Centrale Ferroviaire, Wagons-Lits*

INTERIOR DESIGN AND DECORATION OF COACHES

Gérard Gallet, *Paris*
David Miles, *VS-O-E*
Jim Parks, *VS-O-E*
Stephen Kunze, *VS-O-E*
Jean-Michel Ley, *Assistant to Gallet*
John Sleep, *VS-O-E, Charles Dorin Partnership*
Bob Dunn, *Chelmsford; marquetry*
Marjorie Knowles; *mosaic floors of Pullman lavatories*
Gillian Drury *(Sutcliffe Bros); chairs*
Best & Lloyd, *Birmingham; Pullman lamps, torch light fittings*
Firth Carpets; *carpets*
British Replin, *Ayr; many of the fabrics in the trains*

COLLECTION VENICE SIMPLON-ORIENT-EXPRESS

Paul Bianchini, *Manager of Collection VS-O-E, Paris*
Gérard Gallet, *Designer*
Pierre Fix-Masseau; *posters, book cover*

ORGANISATION OF TRAINS

Colin Bather, *Sea Containers Group, General Manager of Leisure Division*
Claude Ginella, *VS-O-E General Manager*

UK
Peter Rozee, *in charge of UK train operation*
David Williams, *sales & reservations*
Prue Leith, *catering*

Continent
Edouard Ruchti, *Assistant General Manager*
Michel Ranvier, *Executive Chef*

Special events, Pullman chartering and security
Col Anthony Poynder

PUBLICITY

Marketing theme
James Sherwood

Marketing manager
Hugh Thomas (*world-wide*)
David Picken (*USA*)

Brochure
Vernon Stratton, Peter Stillwell, *Vernon Stratton (Advertising) Ltd, London*

Promotional film
Geoff Gale, *Purchasepoint, London*

PUBLIC RELATIONS

UK
Billy Hamilton Public Relations Ltd, *London*
Thelma Stevenson, *Director of Public Relations, VS-O-E*
Christopher Holt, *Publicity and Design Manager, VS-O-E*
Christopher Perkin, *Photographic, VS-O-E*

USA
Bill Galvin, Theodora Simmons,
Carl Byoir & Associates Inc., New York
Mary Homi Public Relations, New York

Continent
Adil Iskaros, *A. N. Iskaros, Paris*
Wilma Salvini, *Milan*

Far East
Tom Hara, *Ozma Public Relations Co. Ltd, Tokyo*

KEY DATES

1843 28 June. The South Eastern Railway opened the first line between London Bridge and Folkestone.

1844 Gladstone's Railway Act dictated that passengers must be provided with seats and protection from the weather.
The South Eastern Railway opened the main line to Dover.

1848 Public train services were started between Paris and Boulogne, Dieppe, Calais and Dunkirk.

1850s Lavatories introduced for first-class passengers.

1861 26 October. The first train went onto the completed Admiralty Pier at Dover.

1869 Nagelmackers visited the USA, saw Pullman's luxury cars.

1872 Nagelmackers built the first five European sleeping cars and formed the Compagnie Internationale de Wagons-Lits on 4 October in Liège.

1873 4 January. Nagelmackers joined forces with Colonel William Mann and began a regular sleeping car service on the Ostend–Cologne, Ostend–Berlin lines on 15 June.
15 February. George Pullman met Midland Railway shareholders who agreed to his operating luxury cars for a supplement to the fare.
The first two Pullman cars were assembled at Derby (*Midland* and *Excelsior*).

1874 21 March. The first meal was served on a British train (in *Victoria*).

1876 Nagelmackers bought out Mann and on 4 December founded the present Compagnie Internationale des Wagons-Lits in Brussels.

1880 Nagelmackers began trials on sleeping cars constructed on bogies and produced the first carriage in Europe with a special area for eating.

1881 The first custom-built Wagon-Restaurant went into service for Wagons-Lits.
5 December. The first all-Pullman train, the Pullman Limited Express, ran from London to Brighton, and was the first train lit by electricity.
The Pullman Palace Car Company was registered in England.

1882 Calais Port was improved to allow sailings independent of the tides.
10 October. The first train of Wagons-Lits sleepers and a restaurant car was displayed in Paris, bound for Vienna.

1883 February. A conference held in Constantinople negotiated the introduction of a train to the East.
4 October. Official inauguration of the Express d'Orient from Paris to Constantinople.

1888 13 August. The through run from Paris to Constantinople was established (67 hours 35 minutes).
Two rival Club Train services began from London to Dover comprising Wagons-Lits saloons.

1891 The Express d'Orient was officially renamed the Orient Express.

1903 27 June. *The Queen* became the first cross-Channel turbine steamer.

1906 The Simplon Tunnel was completed.
The Simplon Express started, from Paris to Milan.
Construction began on Milan Central railway station.

1907 The Simplon Express was extended to Venice.
Davidson Dalziel bought the British Pullman Company.
The brown and cream livery was introduced.

1912 The Simplon Express was extended to Trieste.

1913 The journey London–Dover–Paris took only six and a half hours; this has not been bettered since.

1914 The outbreak of war stopped all Wagons-Lits services in France, Germany, Austria, Serbia and Turkey.

1916 The Germans formed the Mitropa railway company using the Wagons-Lits fleet trapped in Germany.

1919 11 April. André Noblemaire inaugurated th Simplon-Orient-Express on a route laid down by the Allies in the Treaty of Versailles.
Cross-Channel civilian traffic was resumed and the Nord Railway began reconstructing its tracks in the battle zone.

1919 A fleet of 161 Wagons-Lits cars in Russia was taken over without compensation following the Russian revolution.

1922 The first metal-framed blue sleeping cars appeared on the Calais Mediterranée Express.

1923 1 January. Britain's railways were rationalised into four geographical groupings.
10 September. The last railway paddle steamer was withdrawn from the Channel crossing.

1924 14 November. An all-Pullman boat train express started from London to Dover.

1926 13 September. Lord Dalziel gained a controlling interest in the Wagons-Lits Company. He began the Flèche d'Or from Calais to Paris – an all-Pullman service.

1929 15 May. The Golden Arrow Limited was inaugurated with its own ferry, the *Canterbury*, from Victoria to Dover to link with the Flèche d'Or.

1930 The Simplon-Orient-Express was extended to Aleppo in Asia Minor.

1932 Second-class Pullmans were added to the Flèche d'Or, whose livery was changed to blue and cream.
Milan Central station was completed.

1936 14 October. Night Ferry service was started.

1938 18 January. The French railways were nationalised.
Austria was annexed by Germany. Mitropa took over all Wagons-Lits services in Austria and Czechoslovakia.

1939 3 September. The Golden Arrow, the Night Ferry and the Orient-Express were immediately suspended following the declaration of war.

1940 Mitropa took over Wagons-Lits services in Holland, Belgium and parts of France.
The Simplon-Orient-Express was suspended.

1945 8 May. End of World War II. Wagons-Lits had lost 845 cars from their 1939 fleet of 1,738. In Britain Pullman had owned about 200, of which half were damaged and four completely obliterated.

In October cross-Channel services were resumed.

1946 January. The Simplon-Orient-Express began again from Paris to Istanbul.
15 April. The Golden Arrow and Flèche d'Or began, again connected by the ferry *Canterbury*.

1947 The Night Ferry was reinstated.
Internal Wagons-Lits services ceased in Yugoslavia.

1948 18 January. The railways in Britain were nationalised (but not the Pullman Car Company).
The Orient-Express was extended to Czechoslovakia.
1 June. Internal Wagons-Lits services stopped in Romania.

1949 1 October. Wagons-Lits operations ceased in Hungary.

1950 The Flèche d'Or was combined with the ordinary 'rapide' for Paris.
Wagons-Lits contracts expired in Bulgaria.
1 October. The Communists stopped all internal Wagons-Lits services in Czechoslovakia.

1951 1 June. A new Golden Arrow rake was displayed to celebrate the Festival of Britain.
The Turkish border was closed.

1952 The through journey Paris–Istanbul was restored via Yugoslavia and Greece.

1961 11 June. The last steam-hauled Golden Arrow left Victoria.

1969 Pullman cars were withdrawn from the Flèche d'Or.

1972 30 October. Last run of the Golden Arrow.

1977 19 May. Last departure of the Direct-Orient-Express/Marmara-Express for Istanbul.
8 October. Monte Carlo sale of five Wagons-Lits. Two were bought by James B. Sherwood, President of the Sea Containers Group.

1980 31 October. The Night Ferry was withdrawn.

1982 25 May. The inaugural run of the Venice Simplon-Orient-Express from Victoria to Venice introducing a thrice-weekly return service.

BIBLIOGRAPHIES

HISTORY OF THE ORIENT-EXPRESS AND LUXURY TRAINS

Barsley, Michael,
  The Orient Express,
  Stein and Day, New York, 1967
Behrend, George,
  Pullman in Europe,
  Ian Allan, 1962
  Grand European Expresses,
  George Allen and Unwin, London, 1962
  and Kelly, Vincent,
  Vatakli Vagon: Turkish Steam Travel,
  Jersey Artists, Jersey, 1969
  History of Trains de Luxe,
  Transport Publishing Company, Glossop, England,
  1977
Betjeman, John and Gay, John,
  London's Historic Railway Stations,
  John Murray, London, 1972
Briggs, Asa,
  The Power of Steam,
  Michael Joseph, London, 1982
Commault, Roger,
  Georges Nagelmackers, Editions de La Capitelle,
  Uzes (Gard), France, 1972
Cook, Chris,
  A History of the Great Trains,
  Weidenfeld & Nicolson, London, 1977
Cookridge, E.H.,
  *Orient Express, The Life and Times of the World's
  Most Famous Train*,
  Random House, New York, 1978
Des Cars, Jean,
  Sleeping Story,
  Julliard, Paris, 1976
  L'Aventure Des Chemins De Fer,
  André Barret, Paris, 1978

Green, Roger,
  The Train,
  Oxford University Press, Oxford, 1982
Hamilton Ellis, C.,
  The Royal Trains,
  Routledge & Kegan Paul, London, 1975
  Railway Art,
  Ash & Grant Ltd, London, 1977
Hasenson, A.,
  The Golden Arrow,
  Howard Baker, London, 1970
Husband, Joseph,
  The Story of the Pullman Car,
  A.C.McClurg & Co.,Chicago, 1917
Nock, O.S.,
  World Atlas of Railways,
  Intercontinental Book Productions, Rand McNally
  & Co., Maidenhead, England, 1978
Page, Martin,
  The Lost Pleasures of the Great Trains,
  Weidenfeld & Nicolson, London, 1975
Poirot, Fernand,
  Des Wagons et des Hommes,
  Editions Midi-Livre, Toulouse, 1973
Rees, Gareth,
  Early Railway Prints,
  Phaidon Press Ltd, Oxford, 1980
Thomas, R.H.G.,
  The Liverpool & Manchester Railway,
  B.T.Batsford Ltd, London, 1980
Winchester, Clarence (Ed.),
  'The Orient Express', 'Milan Central Station',
  'International Sleeping Cars', 'The Simplon
  Tunnel', in
  Railway Wonders of the World, vols. 1 and 2,
  The Amalgamated Press Ltd, London

FICTION

Ambler, Eric,
  The Mask of Dimitrios,
  Hodder & Stoughton, London, 1939
Christie, Agatha,
  Murder on the Orient Express,
  Collins, London, 1934
Dekobra, Maurice
  La Madone des Sleepings (The Madonna of the
  Sleeping Cars),
  Bestseller Library, Paul Elek, London 1959. First
  published 1925
Den Doolard, A.,
  Express to the East,
  translated by David de Jong, Arthur Barker,
  London, 1936
Fleming, Ian,
  From Russia With Love,
  Jonathan Cape, London, 1957
Green, Graham,
  Stamboul Train,
  Heinemann, London, 1932
Lawrence, D.H.,
  Lady Chatterley's Lover,
  Pan, London, 1970
Roberts, Cecil,
  Victoria Four-Thirty,
  Hodder & Stoughton, London, 1937
White, Ethel Lina,
  The Wheel Spins,
  Collins, London, 1936

FILMS

The Orient-Express has been an inspiration for film-makers no less than for novelists. The following are perhaps the most famous films in which the Orient-Express has starred, sometimes with cars now running in the Venice Simplon-Orient-Express playing a role.

The Lady Vanishes: (1938)
Directed by Alfred Hitchcock.
The entire film takes place on the Orient-Express as it travels to Istanbul. Starring Margaret Lockwood, Michael Redgrave and Dame May Whitty, it was based on Ethel Lina White's novel *The Wheel Spins*. This film's huge success encouraged Hitchcock to pursue the genre in *Night Train to Munich* and *Crook's Tour*. A 1976 re-make starred Cybil Shepherd, Donald Sutherland and Arthur Lowe.

From Russia With Love: (1963)
Directed by Terence Young.
James Bond (Sean Connery), having stolen a 'Lektor' decoding device from the Soviet Embassy in Istanbul, boards the Orient-Express to return to London. Tatiana (Daniela Bianchi), an alluring Russian S.M.E.R.S.H. agent, is fleeing to the West with Bond, but both are unaware that their companion, Red Grant (Robert Shaw), is a ruthless killer for S.P.E.C.T.R.E. with orders to capture the 'Lektor'. The plot works towards its conclusion during this train journey. Lotte Lenya plays the brutal and sinister Rosa Klebb. The YUB sleeping cars used in this film are identical to the staff cars now on the Venice Simplon-Orient-Express.

Murder on the Orient Express: (1974)
Directed by Sidney Lumet.
This is the film version of the Agatha Christie novel of the same name. The 'whodunnit' plot is unravelled in the self-contained world of the snow-bound train somewhere in the Balkans. Hercule Poirot (Albert Finney), coincidentally, is on board ready to question the star-studded list of suspects. The Wagons-Lits restaurant car used in this film was bought by the King of Morocco at the 1977 Monte Carlo auction. The Pullman in the film (4163) has the same Lalique glass panels as 4141 in the VS-O-E. The sleeper was designed by Nelson (similar to 3552, 3553 and 3555 in the VS-O-E).

Agatha: (1976)
Directed by Michael Apted.
After disappearing to Harrogate Spa, the eponymous Agatha Christie (Vanessa Redgrave) meets her husband for a reconciliation at Harrogate Station, where a train of Pullman cars (including *Cygnus*, *Perseus* and *Zena*) waits. Dustin Hoffman plays the tireless reporter who tracks her down.

The Seven Percent Solution: (1979)
Directed by Herbert Ross.
Sherlock Holmes (Nicol Williamson), in Vienna to be cured of his cocaine addiction by Sigmund Freud (Alan Arkin), becomes interested in the case of the beautiful Lola (Vanessa Redgrave) after she has attempted suicide in suspicious circumstances. Lola, mistress of an arrogant baron, is given to a Turkish pasha in settlement of a gambling debt, and is abducted in the pasha's private car attached to the Orient-Express. Holmes pursues the speeding train to effect a rescue.

VENICE

Guide Books

Honour, Hugh,
  The Companion Guide to Venice,
  Collins, London, 1977
Links, J.G.,
  Venice For Pleasure,
  The Bodley Head, London, 1966
Shaw-Kennedy, R.,
  Art and Architecture in Venice,
  Sidgwick & Jackson, London, 1972
Lorenzetti, Giulio,
  Venice and Its Lagoon,
  Edizione Lint, Trieste, 1975 (very detailed)

Background

Grundy, Milton,
  Venice An Anthology Guide,
  Lund Humphries, London; International Monetary Fund for Monuments Inc., New York, 1971
Morris, James,
  Venice,
  Faber & Faber, London, 1974
Norwich, John Julius,
  Venice, The Rise to Empire,
  Allen Lane, London, 1977
  Venice, The Greatness and the Fall,
  Allen Lane, London, 1981
Roiter, Fulvio
  Oriente di Venezia
  Dagor Books, Padova, Italy, 1982

QUESTIONS MOST OFTEN ASKED ABOUT THE TRAIN

Cost of VS-O-E project
£11 million

How many carriages
UK 8 Pullmans, 2 baggage cars
Continent 4 day cars, 11 sleeping cars, 2 staff cars

Length
UK 200 metres + locomotive 25 metres
Continent 401 metres + 2 locomotives 50 metres
each, total 0.5 kilometres

Weight
UK 382 tonnes (+ locomotive 70 tonnes)
Continent 944 tonnes (+ locomotives 360 tonnes)

Time of journey London–Venice
UK 1.5 hours; ferry 1.5 hours;
Continent 19 hours; total 24 hours.

Total distance
1,491 kilometres (926 miles).

Number of seats in British Pullmans
194

Number of passengers per trip
With 11 sleeping cars in the continental rake the
capacity is theoretically 194 – but some are travelling
singly so the maximum carried is generally 176.

Passengers carried 25 May–31 December 1982
21,000.

Nationality of passengers carried during first season
British 39%; American 36%; French 12%; Italian
9%; Japanese 2%; Australian 1%; Belgian 1%

*Passengers who travel the full journey
between London and Venice*
81.3%.

Number of staff
On the continental train there are 40, including:
1 train manager, 1 restaurant manager, 3 head
waiters, 3 chefs du rang, 3 commis waiters, 1
restaurant cashier, 6 chefs, 4 dish-washers,
1 technician, 1 cleaner and 11 cabin attendants (one
per car). During the peak season there are as many as
3 teams. They are backed up by a staff of 28 for
maintenance and preparing the train. In Paris 20 staff
handle reservations, administration and marketing
and 5 prepare food in the kitchen at Austerlitz.
Italian reservations and marketing are handled by 7
staff. There are 2 hostesses in Paris Austerlitz, Milan
Central and Venice Santa Lucia stations and 4 cross
on the ferry with the UK train manager.

Drink consumed on a continental one-way trip
300 drinks served in the bar, 90 bottles of wine and
30 bottles of champagne.

Found on the train
A number of valuable objects have been found and
returned including a roll of $7,000 in cash, a Kruger
Rand and a grey lace bra.

British Pullman Tours and Private Hire
In addition to the regular departures of the Venice
Simplon-Orient-Express from Victoria to Venice,
passengers can travel in the Pullmans to beautiful
and historic places in the British Isles. The day tours
include visits to Leeds Castle, Hever Castle and
Beaulieu. It is also possible to organise trips for
special occasions, like the bankers who went to
Blenheim Palace or the private party who took the
train to Goodwood for a day at the races.

Telephone enquiries
UK (01)-928 5837
USA (800)-223 1588 (Nationwide)
(212)-661 4540 (New York)
France (1)-256 1750
Italy (02)-6703153 (Milan)
(041)-30603/85811 (Venice)

PHOTOGRAPHIC ACKNOWLEDGMENTS

The author and publishers would like to thank the following people for providing and giving permission to reproduce the pictures in this book:

(Every effort has been made to trace copyright owners; if any have been omitted we will be glad to remedy this in future editions on receipt of the relevant information.)

Page

Frontispiece Sea Containers Photographic Library, London
4 Sea Containers/Julian Simmonds – Xenon Photos
10 *top left* Compagnie Internationale des Wagons-Lits, Paris
10 *top right* Wagons-Lits
10 *bottom left* Weidenfeld and Nicolson Archives, London
10 *bottom right* Radio Times Hulton Picture Library, London
10 *centre* Sea Containers/Dimitri Kasterine
13 Sea Containers/Chris Perkin
14 Sea Containers
16 *left* Illustrated London News Picture Library, London
16 *right* Museum of British Transport
17 Weidenfeld and Nicolson Archives
18 Sea Containers
19 From *History of Trains de Luxe* by George Behrend, The Transport Publishing Company, Glossop
20 Millbrook House Picture Library
21 *top* Sea Containers
21 *bottom* Press Association, London
22 Wagons-Lits
23 La Vie du Rail, Paris
24 Wagons-Lits
25 *insert* Popperfoto, London
25 The Bettmann Archive, New York
26 Sea Containers
27 *top* Mary Evans Picture Library, London
27 *bottom* Mary Evans Picture Library
28 Wagons-Lits
29 La Vie du Rail
30 Associated Press, London
30 *insert* The Bettmann Archive
31 Sea Containers
32 Wagons-Lits
33 Associated Press
34 Sea Containers/Julian Simmonds – Xenon Photos
36 Fox Photos, London
37 *left* Sea Containers
37 *right* Sea Containers
38 Sea Containers/Eric Guilliam
39 *left* Sea Containers/Mrs A.Jones Collection, Birchington-on-Sea
39 *right* Sea Containers/Julian Simmonds –

Xenon Photos
40 *left* Sea Containers/Chris Perkin
40 *right* Sea Containers/Mrs A.Jones Collection
41 *left* Sea Containers/Chris Perkin
41 *right* Press Association
42 *top left* Sea Containers/Mrs A. Jones Collection
42 *bottom left* Sea Containers/Chris Perkin
42 *right* Sea Containers
43 Radio Times Hulton Picture Library
44 Sea Containers/Mrs A. Jones Collection
45 Sea Containers/Chris Perkin
46 Author's photograph
47 Photo Harlangue-Viollet, Paris
48 Mrs Beth Vinding Collection, Sweden
49 Sea Containers/Chris Perkin
50 Illustrated London News Picture Library
51 The Mansell Collection, London
52 *top* Sea Containers/Chris Perkin
52 *bottom* Wagons-Lits
53 *top* Sea Containers/Chris Perkin
53 *bottom* La Vie du Rail
54 *top* Sea Containers
54 *bottom* Sea Containers
55 Wagons-Lits
56 Sea Containers/Chris Perkin
57 *top* Wagons-Lits
57 *bottom* Wagons-Lits
58 Sea Containers/Pierre Vanhoutte
59 Sea Containers/Chris Perkin
60 *left* Sea Containers/Chris Perkin
60 *right* La Vie Du Rail
61 Sea Containers/Chris Perkin
62 Thorn-EMI Films Ltd., London
63 *top left* Sea Containers/Chris Perkin
63 *right* Lords Gallery, London
64 Sea Containers/Chris Perkin
66 The Bettmann Archive
67 Sea Containers/Pierre Vanhoutte
68 La Vie du Rail
69 Sea Containers/Chris Perkin
70 Sea Containers/Pierre Vanhoutte
74 Sea Containers/Julian Simmonds – Xenon Photos
75 Nice Matin, Nice
76 Nice Matin, Nice
77 *left* Sea Containers/Lord Garnock Collection

77 *right* Sea Containers/Bill McAlpine Collection
78 Sea Containers/David Lowther Collection
79 Sea Containers
80 Sea Containers
81 Sea Containers
82 *left* Sea Containers/Eric Guilliam
82 *right* Sea Containers/Chris Perkin
83 Sea Containers/Eric Guilliam
84 Sea Containers/Chris Perkin
85 Sea Containers/Julian Simmonds – Xenon Photos
86 *left* Sea Containers/Mike Hughes
86 *right* Sea Containers/Mike Hughes
87 Sea Containers/Chris Perkin
88 *left* Sea Containers/Chris Perkin
88 *right* Sea Containers/Eric Guilliam
89 Sea Containers/Chris Perkin
90 Sea Containers/Eric Guilliam
91 Sea Containers
92 Sea Containers/Roland.
93 Sea Containers
96 Sea Containers/Chris Perkin
97 Sea Containers
98 Sea Containers/Chris Perkin
100 *left* Sea Containers
100 *right* Sea Containers
101 *left* Sea Containers/Paul Bianchini
101 *right* Private Collection, Paris
102 Sea Containers
103 Sea Containers
104 Sea Containers
105 *left* Sea Containers
105 *right* Sea Containers
106 Sea Containers/Pierre Vanhoutte
108 Sea Containers
109 Sea Containers/Adil Iskaros
111 *top* Wagons-Lits
111 *bottom* Sea Containers
112 Sea Containers/Dimitri Kasterine
114 Sea Containers
115 Sea Containers/Mike Hughes
117 Gamma/Peccoux, Paris
118 Sea Containers
120 Author's Collection
121 *left* Sea Containers/Chris Perkin
121 *right* Sea Containers/Dimitri Kasterine
122 Sea Containers/Dimitri Kasterine

123 Sea Containers/Chris Perkin
124 *left* Sea Containers
124 *right* Sea Containers/Dimitri Kasterine
125 Sea Containers/copyright JAK
126 Sea Containers
127 Sea Containers
128 *left* Sea Containers/Chris Perkin
128 *right* Sea Containers/Chris Perkin
129 Sea Containers/Julian Simmonds – Xenon Photos
130 Sea Containers/Ralph Gobits
131 Sea Containers/Dimitri Kasterine
132 *top* Sea Containers/Dimitri Kasterine
132 *bottom* Sea Containers/Dimitri Kasterine
133 Sea Containers/Dimitri Kasterine
134 Sea Containers
135 Sea Containers/Derek Richard
136 Sea Containers
137 *left* Photograph by Bruce Brown. Reproduced from Vogue. Copyright the Condé Nast Publications Ltd., London
137 *top right* Sea Containers/Dimitri Kasterine
137 *bottom right* Photograph by Bruce Brown. Reproduced from Vogue. Copyright The Condé Nast Publications Ltd., London
138 *left* Robert Harding Picture Library/S.H. and D.H.Cavanaugh
138 *right* Radio Times hulton Picture Library
139 Popperfoto
140 Sea Containers
141 Sea Containers/Chris Perkin
142 *left* From *La Stazione Centrale di Milano*, Di Baio Editore, Milan
142 *right* Sea Containers/Dimitri Kasterine
143 Sea Containers
144 Sea Containers/Chris Perkin
145 Sea Containers/Chris Perkin
146 Sea Containers/Ralph Gobits
147 Author's Photograph
148 Sea Containers
149 Author's photograph
150 Sea Containers

INDEX